Living Through the
Sexual Revolution

Other books in the Living Through the Cold War series:

Living Through the
Sexual Revolution

Aaron J. LaDuke, Book Editor

GREENHAVEN PRESS
An imprint of Thomson Gale, a part of The Thomson Corporation

Detroit • New York • San Francisco • San Diego • New Haven, Conn.
Waterville, Maine • London • Munich

Bonnie Szumski, *Publisher*
Helen Cothran, *Managing Editor*
Scott Barbour, *Series Editor*

© 2006 Thomson Gale, a part of The Thomson Corporation.

For more information, contact:
Greenhaven Press
27500 Drake Rd.
Farmington Hills, MI 48331-3535
Or you can visit our Internet site at http://www.gale.com

LIBRARY OF CONGRESS CATALOGING-IN-PUBLICATION DATA

Living through the sexual revolution / Aaron J. LaDuke, book editor
    p. cm. -- (Living through the Cold War)
    Includes bibliographical references and index. ISBN 0-7377-2913-9 (lib. : alk. paper)
    1. Sex--United States--History--20th century. 2. Sexual ethics--United States--History--20th century. 3. Sex customs--United States--History--20th century. 4. Sex role--United States--History--20th century. I. LaDuke, Aaron J. II. Series.
    HQ18.U5L53 2006
    306.7'0973'0945--dc22
                                      2005052563

Printed in the United States of America
10 9 8 7 6 5 4 3 2 1

Contents

Chapter 1: Early Voices of the Revolution

   Helen Gurley Brown

   In 1962 the best-selling book *Sex and the Single Girl* contradicted the conservative family values of the 1950s
   with its provocative account of the author's active, unmarried lifestyle.

   David Halberstam

   Alfred Kinsey's unprecedented scientific study of human
   sexuality shocked readers by claiming Americans were
   more sexually active than was generally believed.

   Betty Friedan

   The Feminine Mystique claimed that women have difficulty developing full identities because they are confined
   to domestic roles. Many women wrote to the author pas-
   sionately agreeing and disagreeing with her book's
   theory.

Chapter 2: Changes in Sexual Values

   David Allyn

   The Sexual Freedom League was founded in the 1960s to
   brazenly promote the idea of sexual freedom and to oppose conservative values.

   Elizabeth Siegel Watkins

   Approved in 1960, the pill was a convenient, highly controversial form of birth control that allowed women to
   be more sexually active but was also frequently blamed
   for America's deteriorating sexual morality.

Foreword

At the midpoint of the Cold War, in early 1968, U.S. television viewers saw surprising reports from Vietnam, where American ground troops had been fighting since 1965. They learned that South Vietnamese Communist rebels, known as the Vietcong, had attacked unexpectedly throughout the country. At one point Vietcong insurgents engaged U.S. troops and officials in a firefight at the very center of U.S. power in Vietnam, the American embassy in South Vietnam's capital, Saigon. Meanwhile, thousands of soldiers and marines faced a concerted siege at Khe Sanh, an isolated base high in central Vietnam's mountains. Their adversary was not the Vietcong, but rather the regular North Vietnamese army.

Reporters and U.S. citizens quickly learned that these events constituted the Tet Offensive, a coordinated attack by Vietnamese Communists that occurred in late January, the period of Tet, Vietnam's new year. The American public was surprised by the Tet Offensive because they had been led to believe that the United States and its South Vietnamese allies were winning the war, that Vietcong forces were weak and dwindling, and that the massive buildup of American forces (there were some five hundred thousand U.S. troops in Vietnam by early 1968) ensured that the south would remain free of a Communist takeover. Since 1965, politicians, pundits, and generals had claimed that massive American intervention was justified and that the war was being won. On a publicity tour in November 1967 General William Westmoreland, the American commander in Vietnam, had assured officials and reporters that "the ranks of the Vietcong are thinning steadily" and that "we have reached a point where the end begins to come into view." President Lyndon B. Johnson's advisers, meanwhile, continually encouraged him to publicly emphasize "the light at the end of the tunnel."

Ordinary Americans had largely supported the troop buildup in Vietnam, believing the argument that the country was an important front in the Cold War, the global effort to stop the spread of communism that had begun in the late 1940s. Communist regimes already held power in nearby China, North Korea, and in northern Vietnam; it was deemed necessary to hold the line in the south not only to prevent communism from taking hold there but to prevent other nations from falling to communism throughout Asia. In 1965, polls showed that 80 percent of Americans believed that intervention in Vietnam was justified despite the fact that involvement in this fight would alter American life in numerous ways. For example, young men faced the possibility of being drafted and sent to fight—and possibly die—in a war thousands of miles away. As the war progressed, citizens watched more and more of their sons—both draftees and enlisted men—being returned to the United States in coffins (approximately fifty-eight thousand Americans died in Vietnam). Antiwar protests roiled college campuses and sometimes the streets of major cities. The material costs of the war threatened domestic political reforms and America's economic health, offering the continuing specter of rising taxes and shrinking services. Nevertheless, as long as the fight was succeeding, a majority of Americans could accept these risks and sacrifices.

Tet changed many minds, suggesting as it did that the war was not, in fact, going well. When CBS news anchor Walter Cronkite, who was known as "the most trusted man in America," suggested in his broadcast on the evening of February 27 that the Vietnam War might be unwinnable and could only end in a stalemate, many people wondered if he might be right and began to suspect that the positive reports from generals and politicians might have been misleading. It was a turning point in the battle for public opinion. Johnson reportedly said that Cronkite's expressions of doubt signaled the loss of mainstream America's support for the war. Indeed, after Tet more and more people joined Cronkite in wondering whether fighting this obscure enemy in an isolated country halfway around the world was worth the cost—whether it was a truly important front in the Cold War. They made their views known through demonstrations and opinion polls, and politicians were forced to respond. In a dramatic and unexpected turn of events, Johnson declined to run for reelection in 1968, stating that his involvement in the political campaign would detract from his efforts to negotiate a peace agreement with North Vietnam. His successor, Richard Nixon, won the election after promising to end the war.

The Tet Offensive and its consequences provide strong examples of how the Cold War touched the lives of ordinary Americans. Far from being an abstract geopolitical event, the Cold War, as Tet reveals, was an ever-present influence in the everyday life of the nation. Greenhaven Press's Living Through the Cold War series provides snapshots into the lives of ordinary people during the Cold War, as well as their reactions to its major events and developments. Each volume is organized around a particular event or distinct stage of the Cold War. Primary documents such as eyewitness accounts and speeches give firsthand insights into both ordinary peoples' experiences and leaders' decisions. Secondary sources provide factual information and place events within a larger global and historical context. Additional resources include a detailed introduction, a comprehensive chronology, and a thorough bibliography. Also included are an annotated table of contents and a detailed index to help the reader locate information quickly. With these features, the Living Through the Cold War series reveals the human dimension of the superpower rivalry that defined the globe during most of the latter half of the twentieth century.

Introduction

The sexual revolution in America, which occurred from roughly the early 1960s to the early 1980s, was an era characterized by an unprecedented open examination and liberalization of the country's sexual values. Some major events that sparked the sexual revolution were the introduction of the birth control pill, the rising popularity of *Playboy* magazine, and the formation of the National Organization for Women. The paranoid atmosphere of the Cold War between the United States and the Soviet Union encouraged many Americans to conform to the traditional values of church, home, and country; however, during this time passionate voices opposed to these traditional values began to emerge.

Many of these voices came together to form the political and cultural phenomena known as the sexual revolution. On the political side, those in mixed-race marriages, gays and lesbians, and especially women fought with vigilant intensity to bring about legal changes during these two decades. Culturally, many called into question the conservative sexual mores of the fifties. The role of women in society was particularly challenged. In the 1950s women were usually thought of as primarily domestic caregivers. As the sexual revolution of the sixties and seventies wore on, however, women began to be seen as more sexually independent, and the traditional institution of marriage was challenged in the process. The depictions of women in popular novels, television shows, and films provide a useful window through which to examine women's changing social roles during the sexual revolution.

The television series *Leave It to Beaver* illustrated the stereotypical domestic roles for women during the late fifties and early sixties. Running from 1957 to 1963, the series was centered on the Cleaver family, which consisted of father Ward, who worked an unspecified nine-to-five job; mother June, a homemaker; reliable older son Wally; and younger son Theodore (aka the Beaver), a lovable rascal. The plot of most episodes consisted of the Beaver getting into some good-natured trouble that the close-knit family would overcome together by the end of the show. *Leave It to Beaver* enjoyed tremendous popularity because it reassured Americans during the Cold War that life in the suburbs was idyllic and safe. Richard Stengel, a former editor at *Time* magazine, said of the series, "Weekly, the values of middle-class America were tested on the show's half-hour and proved sound. . . . *Leave It to Beaver* is based on a reassuring assumption: the family, solid and resilient, is the ultimate sanctuary from the world."[1] June Cleaver, whom Stengel describes as "forever [emerging] from the kitchen flawlessly coiffed and groomed, carrying a tray of freshly baked cookies,"[2] is the sole caretaker of this sanctuary and is perhaps the most recognized example of the typical 1950s housewife. She is responsible for all the cooking, cleaning, and care of the boys, except when Ward's expertise is required, as Stengel notes, for lawn mowing or a heart-to-heart talk with either Wally or Beaver. *Leave It to Beaver* portrayed precisely the traditional, suburban family perspective against which early proponents of the sexual revolution began to react.

Grace Metalious provided an early contrary voice with her 1956 best-selling novel *Peyton Place*. Metalious's novel attempted to depict female characters as more complicated than domestic caretakers cut from the June Cleaver cloth. *Peyton Place* followed the lives of three women in a small New England town as they came to grips with their identities and their sexuality. Women were depicted as sexually eager, which was shocking to most readers (much as Alfred Kinsey's 1953 book *Sexual Behavior in the Human Female* had surprised Americans by reporting that 50 percent of the women whom Kinsey surveyed had sexual intercourse before marriage). Metalious, besides exposing hypocritical views on women and sexuality, also pursued the dark themes of rape, incest, infidelity, and abortion. Reactions to *Peyton Place* were, and are, mixed. Some have hailed the novel as a valuable corrective to the stereotype of the domestic, acquiescent woman, but others have simply called the book dime-store trash. Beyond question is the fact that novels like Metalious's showed society that female sexuality might be more complicated than most acknowledged.

Robert Rimmer's 1967 novel *The Harrad Experiment* further challenged women's societal roles by openly endorsing group marriage. Set in a New England college, the characters of the novel are student participants in an experiment in which they are assigned to a roommate of the opposite sex, with whom they form a sexual relationship. After a short period, the students are encouraged to switch partners with others in the experiment. In this stage, jealousy often erupts between the students as they maneuver to secure a relationship with the individual they desire; the novel often depicts women as objects that men strive to secure. Finally, participants realize that forming an open group with four or five other couples is better than pursuing a single, monogamous relationship. The goal of the experiment is to abandon the supposed illusions of romantic love and embrace a more scientific approach to sex. Above all, the novel suggests that in monogamous relationships women are reduced to the status of male-owned property. The novel defines promiscuity as the product of a repressed culture. But the novel does not espouse free love and orgies; rather than promoting monogamy or hedonism, the idealistic narrative hopes that, as historian David Allyn observes, "ultimately, sexually liberated men and women would form happy, enduring group marriages, in which jealously and secrecy and adultery and divorce would be unknown."[3] *The Harrad Experiment* was a tremendous success, commercially and politically. Rimmer was invited to join the National Organization for Women by Betty Friedan, the influential author of *The Feminine Mystique* (1963), a book that tried to expose the same repressive aspects of marriage that *The Harrad Experiment* emphasized.

The popular film *Bob and Carol and Ted and Alice* (1969) similarly questioned the institution of marriage by bringing the concept of open marriage to movie theaters. The practice of "swinging," or mate swapping, depicted in the movie, was another way in which the traditional concept of marriage was challenged during the sexual revolution. Swinging involved two couples switching mates for a brief time, usually one night. This sometimes occurred in the form of "key parties," at which husbands would drop their keys into a bowl, and wives would randomly pick the keys of the men that would take them home that evening. Though neither group marriage nor swinging became widespread practices, even in 1960s America, they did present alternatives to marriage, a rarely questioned institution that provided the bedrock for 1950s values.

Erica Jong's 1973 novel *Fear of Flying* pushed hardest against the societal boundaries set for women during the decades of the sexual revolution. The protagonist of Jong's novel is the antithesis of the June Cleaver, 1950s archetypal woman. Jong's character leaves her husband and home to search for the ultimate sexual experience. *Fear of Flying* was completely dedicated to female sexual self-expression, and many felt it enunciated the themes of feminine liberation far more directly and eloquently than Metalious's *Peyton Place* had in 1956. Allyn says that *Fear of Flying* "paved the way for a new era of personal autonomy, sexual self-expression, and freedom from fear. At long last, a woman could, like a man, maximize her opportunities for sexual satisfaction."[4] Jong's novel was strong proof from popular media that sexual boundaries for women had in fact been relaxed by the sexual revolution.

The intensity of the women's movement leveled off after the end of the sexual revolution (which is often attributed to the rise of the AIDS crisis in the early 1980s). However, the changed expectations of women like those presented in *Fear of Flying* continue to be reflected in contemporary television shows such as *Sex and the City.* This sitcom, which ran on the HBO network from 1998 to 2004, is set in New York City and focuses on four female friends in their thirties and forties: Carrie (the show's main character and narrator), a sex columnist; Charlotte, an art dealer with a blue-blood upbringing; Miranda, a more cynical, career-minded lawyer; and Samantha, a brash and fun-loving publicist. The episodes center primarily on the friends' search for worthy mates and graphically portray the sexual encounters they have along the way.

At the same time, though, the series depicts the women as financially and socially independent. James Poniewozik, the TV critic for *Time* magazine, says of *Sex and the City,* "*Sex* became a pop-culture icon for its astute bedroom politics, for the saucy Seinfeld banter (laced with corny double entendres) of its glam foursome, but above all for recognizing that a woman can live well without being at either end of a man's leash."[5] Critics have accused the series of promoting immorality by encouraging a reckless sexual lifestyle. Further, they feel that it is at times simply pornography with a flimsy plot. Others say in response that *Sex and the City* tries to realistically and artistically depict sexual behavior in the urban United States and that it should be praised for featuring strong friendships among women. Poniewozik insists that "*Sex* is no '70s-style war between the sexes. It's a border negotiation over personal space, customs and autonomy. It's an accomplishment that *Sex* holds out the possibility of saying no to changing your life for a man."[6] Certainly *Sex and the City*'s Carrie Bradshaw is a far cry from June Cleaver. Furthermore, the series' wide viewership and numerous Golden Globe and Emmy awards illustrates that since the sexual revolution Americans have become more open to depictions of women as independent and sexually liberated.

Notes

1. Richard Stengel, "When Eden Was in Surburbia," *Time*, August 9, 1982, p. 33.
2. Stengel, "When Eden Was in Surburbia," p. 34.
3. David Allyn, *Make Love, Not War: The Sexual Revolution, an Unfettered History.* New York: Little, Brown, 2000, p. 73.
4. Allyn, *Make Love, Not War*, p. 267.
5. James Poniewozik, "Waiting for Prince Charming," *Time*, August 28, 2000, p. 64.
6. Poniewozik, "Waiting for Prince Charming," p. 65.

LIVING THROUGH
THE COLD WAR

Early Voices of the Revolution

Rethinking the Value of the Single Life for Women

Helen Gurley Brown

Helen Gurley Brown's best-selling book Sex and the Single Girl, *published in 1962, was at the time an extremely provocative account of her life as a single woman that ran contrary to the conservative family values of the fifties. Brown encouraged women to embrace single life and to enjoy multiple sex partners. She also advised women to be more independent, to pay less attention to social constraints, and to be more ambitious in their careers. Ultimately, a quality marriage was still the goal for Brown; however, she was a strong advocate for remaining single longer and relishing the journey toward married life.*

In the following excerpt from the first chapter of her book, Brown challenges preconceived conceptions of single women and also gives a number of detailed suggestions for living a full single life. In addition to Sex and the Single Girl, *Brown wrote its sequel,* Sex and the New Single Girl, *in 1970. Brown also served as editor for* Cosmopolitan *magazine from 1965 to 1997, redirecting the struggling magazine toward single, young career women and promoting the image of the sophisticated, intelligent, and sexually liberated woman.*

Frankly, the magazines and their marriage statistics give me a royal pain.

There is a more important truth that magazines never deal with, that single women are too brainwashed to figure out, that married women know but won't admit, that married men *and* single men endorse in a body, and that is that the single woman, far from being a creature to be pitied and patronized, is emerging as the newest glamour girl of our times.

She is engaging because she lives by her wits. She supports herself. She has had to sharpen her personality and mental resources to a glitter in order to survive in a competitive world and the sharpening looks good. Economically she is a dream. She is not a parasite, a dependent, a scrounger, a sponger or a bum. She is a giver, not a taker, a winner and not a loser.

Why else is she attractive? Because she isn't married, that's why! She is free to be The Girl in a man's life or at least his vision of The Girl, whether he is married or single himself.

When a man thinks of a married woman, no matter how lovely she is, he must inevitably picture her greeting her husband at the door with a martini or warmer welcome, fixing little children's lunches or scrubbing them down because they've fallen into a mudhole. She is somebody else's wife and somebody else's mother.

When a man thinks of a single woman, he pictures her alone in her apartment, smooth legs sheathed in pink silk Capri pants, lying tantalizingly among dozens of satin cushions, trying to read but not very successfully, for *he* is in that room—filling her thoughts, her dreams, her life.

The Advantages of Being Single

Why else is a single woman attractive? She has more time and often more money to spend on herself. She has the extra twenty minutes to exercise every day, an hour to make up her face for their date. She has all day Saturday to whip up a silly, wonderful cotton brocade tea coat to entertain him in next day or hours to find it at a bargain sale.

Besides making herself physically more inviting, she has the freedom to furnish her mind. She can read [French philosopher Marcel] Proust, learn Spanish, study *Time, Newsweek* and *The Wall Street Journal.*

Most importantly, a single woman, even if she is a file clerk, moves in the world of men. She knows their language—the language of retailing, advertising, motion pictures, exporting, shipbuilding. Her world is a far more colorful world than the one of P.T.A. [Parent-Teacher Association], Dr. [Benjamin] Spock [child care expert] and the jammed clothes dryer.

A single woman never has to drudge. She can get her housework over within one good hour Saturday morning plus one other hour to iron blouses and white collars. She need never break her fingernails or her spirit waxing a playroom or cleaning out the garage.

She has more money for clothes and for trips than any but a wealthily married few.

Sex and the Single Life

Theoretically a "nice" single woman has no sex life. What nonsense! She has a better sex life than most of her married friends. She need never be bored with one man per lifetime. Her choice of partners is endless and they seek *her.* They never come to her bed duty-bound. Her married friends refer to her pursuers as wolves, but actually many of them turn out to be lambs—to be shorn and worn by her.

Sex of course is more than the act of coitus. It begins with the delicious feeling of attraction between two people. It may never go further, but sex it is. And a single woman may promote the attraction, bask in the sensation, drink it like wine and pour it over her like blossoms, with never a guilty twinge. She can promise with a look, a touch, a letter or a kiss—and she doesn't have to deliver. She can be maddeningly hypocritical and, after arousing desire, insist that it be shut off by stating she wants to be chaste for the man she marries. Her pursuer may strangle her with his necktie, but he can't *argue* with her. A flirtatious married woman is expected to Go Through With Things.

Since for a female getting there is at *least* half the fun, a single woman has reason to prize the luxury of taking long, gossamer, attenuated, pulsating trips before finally arriving in bed. A married woman and her husband have precious little time and energy for romance after they've put the house, animals and children to bed. A married woman with her lover is on an even tighter schedule.

During and after an affair, a single woman suffers emotional stress. Do you think a married woman can bring one off more blissfully free of strain? (One of my close friends, married, committed suicide over a feckless lover. Another is currently in a state of fingernail-biting hysteria.) And I would rather be the other woman than the woman who watches a man *stray* from her.

Yet, while indulging her libido, which she has plenty of if she is young and healthy, it is still possible for the single woman to be a lady, to be highly respected and even envied if she is successful in her work.

I did it. So have many of my friends.

Making the Best of It

Perhaps this all sounds like bragging. I do not mean to suggest for a moment that being single is not often hell. But I do mean to suggest that it can also be quite heavenly, whether you choose *it* or it chooses *you.*

There is a catch to achieving single bliss. You have to work like a son of a bitch.

But show me the married woman who can loll about and eat cherry bonbons! Hourly she is told by every magazine she reads what she must do to keep her marriage from bursting at the seams. There is no peace for anybody married *or* single unless you do your chores. Frankly, I wouldn't want to make the choice between a married hell or a single hell. They're both hell.

However, serving time as a single woman can give you the foundation for a better marriage if you finally go that route. Funnily enough it also gives you the choice.

How to Live the Good Life

What then does it take for a single woman to lead the rich, full life?

Here is what it *doesn't* take.

Great beauty. A man seems not so much attracted to overwhelming beauty as he is just overwhelmed by it—at first. Then he grows accustomed to the face, fabulous as it is, and starts to explore the personality. Now the hidden assets of an *attractive* girl can be as fascinating as the dark side of the moon. Plumbing the depths of a raving beauty may be like plumbing the depths of Saran Wrap.

What it also doesn't take to collect men is money. Have you ever noticed the birds who circle around rich girls? Strictly for the aviary.

You also don't have to be Auntie Mame and electrify everybody with your high-voltage personality. Do *you* like the girl who always grabs the floor to tell what happened to *her* in the elevator? Well neither does anybody else.

And you don't have to be the fireball who organizes bowling teams, gets out the chain letters and makes certain *somebody* gives a shower for the latest bride.

Working on You

What you do have to do is work with the raw material you have, namely you, and never let up.

If you would like the good single life—since the married life is not just now forthcoming—you can't afford to leave any facet of you unpolished.

You don't have to do anything brassy or show-offy or against your nature. Your most prodigious work will be on *you*—at home. (When I got married, I moved in with six-pound dumbbells, slant board, an electronic device for erasing wrinkles, several pounds of soy lecithin, powdered calcium and yeast-liver concentrate for Serenity Cocktails and enough high-powered vitamins to generate life in a statue.)

Unlike Madame Bovary you don't chase the glittering life, you lay a trap for it. You tunnel up from the bottom.

You *do* need a quiet, private, personal aggression . . . a refusal to take singleness lying down. A sweetly smiling drop-dead attitude for the marrying Sams, and that means *you too.*

Your Own Style

You must develop style. Every girl has one . . . it's just a case of getting it out in the open, caring for it and feeding it like an orchid until it leafs out. (One girl is a long-legged, tennis-playing whiz by day, a serene pool at night for friends to drown their tensions in. Wholesomeness is her trademark. A petite brunette is gamine but serious-minded. A knockout in black jersey, she is forever promoting discussions on [French writer] Stendhal or diminishing colonialism. An intellectual charmer.)

Brains are an asset but it doesn't take brainy brains like a nuclear physicist's. Whatever it is that keeps you from saying anything unkind and keeps you asking bright questions even when you don't quite understand the answers will do nicely. A lively interest in people and things (even if you aren't *that* interested) is why bosses trust you with new assignments, why men talk to you at parties . . . and sometimes ask you out to dinner.

Fashion is your powerful ally. Let the "secure" married girls eschew shortening their skirts (or lengthening them) and wear their classic cashmeres and tweeds until everybody could throw up. You be the girl other girls look at to see what America has copied from Paris.

Final Suggestions

Roommates are for sorority girls. You need an apartment alone even if it's over a garage.

Your figure can't harbor an ounce of baby fat. It never looked good on anybody but babies.

You must cook well. It will serve you faithfully.

You must have a job that interests you, at which you work hard.

I say "must" about all these things as though you were under orders. You don't have to do anything. I'm just telling you what worked for me.

I'm sure of this. You're not too fat, too thin, too tall, too small, too dumb, or too myopic to have married women gazing at you wistfully.

This then is not a study on how to get married but how to stay single—in superlative style.

Alfred Kinsey Reports on America's Sexual Practices

David Halberstam

Alfred Kinsey's unprecedented scientific study of human sexuality and his resulting books, Sexual Behavior in the Human Male *(1948) and* Sexual Behavior in the Human Female *(1953), had a profound effect on the social and cultural values of the United States in the 1950s and 1960s. Kinsey's work is widely accepted as one of the main causes of the sexual revolution.*

The best-selling Sexual Behavior in the Human Male *shocked readers by claiming that men's sex lives were much more active and varied than was commonly believed. A sampling of some of Kinsey's statistics that challenged people's conceptions of sexual behavior in the 1950s include the following: Ninety-two percent of men and boys masturbate; by age twenty, over 70 percent of unmarried men have had sexual intercourse; and 10 percent of adult males are exclusively homosexual for a period of three years during their lives. Most controversial were Kinsey's comments about homosexuality; during a period when psychiatry was dominated by those who believed homosexuals were mentally disturbed, Kinsey believed that homosexuality was just another outlet for male sexuality.*

Both of Kinsey's books were met with mixed reactions. Some attacked Kinsey's methods while others accused him of contributing to the decline of morality in America. Some of Kinsey's claims about women were particularly controversial, such as the finding that married women who had premarital sex had more orgasms after they were married and that lesbians were better at inducing orgasms in other women than were men. These results generated so much animosity that some began to claim that Kinsey was trying to weaken American morals to make way for a

Communist takeover. Though the claims were false, they were persuasive enough to end Kinsey's research grant.

The following selection chronicles what it was like for Kinsey to conduct the first scientific study of sex within the conservative years of the late forties and early fifties. The article highlights the tremendous resistance Kinsey met with in a pre–sexual revolution America. The author, David Halberstam, is a highly respected journalist, historian, and sportswriter who won a Pulitzer Prize for his book The Best and the Brightest, *a fierce indictment of Robert McNamara, secretary of defense during the Vietnam War.*

Alfred Kinsey was both fascinated and troubled by the vast difference between American sexual behavior the society wanted to believe existed and American sexual practices as they actually did exist. For example, at least 80 percent of successful businessmen, his interviews showed, had had extramarital affairs. "God," he noted, "what a gap between social front and reality!" And he spent the latter part of his career tearing away the facade that Americans used to hide their sexual selves.

Kinsey was no bohemian. He lived in the Midwest, he married the first woman he ever dated, and he stayed married to her for his entire life. Because he was an entomologist and loved to collect bugs, he and his bride went camping on their honeymoon. In his classes at . . . Indiana [University] he always sported a bow tie and a crew cut. He drove the same old Buick for most of his lifetime and was immensely proud of the fact that he had more than a hundred thousand miles on it. On Sundays he and his wife invited faculty and graduate-student friends to their home to listen to records of classical music. . . .

He seemed . . . to be the least likely candidate to become one of the most controversial figures of his generation. He was a highly respected professor of zoology in a good department at Indiana University. Esteemed by his colleagues for his collection of gall wasps, he was also popular with his students, a kind and humane teacher who was generous with his time.

Then, in 1938, a group of his students came to him and asked questions about marriage. He was touched by their innocence. At first he refrained from answering, fearing he knew too little. Then he went out and read everything he could on the subject and was appalled by the available material—in both quantity and quality. Some of the students petitioned the university to start a course on sexuality and marriage. From the start it was Kinsey's course. He was one of eight faculty members who taught it, and he gave three of the basic lectures. The course was a huge success. It soon became an obsession with him. Clara Kinsey was known on occasion to tell friends, "I hardly see him at night any more since he took up sex." . . .

Becoming a Sex Researcher

He began by taking the sexual histories of his students. He conducted the interviews in his tiny office, where he locked the door and sent his assistant elsewhere. The enrollment for the class grew every year; before long four hundred students were signing up for it. But his heart was in the research. Soon he was not only taking the sexual histories of his students but traveling out of town on weekends to find additional subjects. As the project took an increasing amount of his time, there was an inevitable conservative reaction against him in Indiana.

In 1940 Herman Wells, the president of Indiana University, who was largely sympathetic to Kinsey and his work, called him in and, citing complaints from local ministers, told him that he would have to make a choice: He could either teach the course or take his histories, but he could not do both. Wells assumed that Kinsey would give up the case histories. Kinsey resigned from the course. Those who thought he would do otherwise, he noted, "do not know me." From then on he devoted himself exclusively to his research. . . .

During the forties, while much of the rest of the country was going off to war, Alfred Kinsey and a handful of assistants set off to interview as many men and women as they could on their sexual habits. At first they had limited resources; Kinsey used part of his own small salary to hire others.

In 1941 he got his first grant from a foundation, for sixteen hundred dollars; in 1943 he received his first grant from the Medical Sciences Division of the Rockefeller Foundation, a gift of twenty-three thousand dollars; by 1947 that figure was forty thousand dollars. The foundation thereby became the principal financial backer of his studies. By 1947 he was preparing to publish the first book of his results—a simple report on the human animal studied in one of its highest-priority biologic acts. His conclusions do not seem particularly startling today: that healthy sex led to a healthy marriage; that there was more extramarital sex on the part of both men and women than they wanted to admit; that petting and premarital sex tended to produce better marriages; that masturbation did not cause mental problems, as superstition held; that there was more homosexuality than people wanted to admit.

Publishing the Report

President Wells had made a few minor requests of him: He asked Kinsey not to publish during the sixty-one days that the Indiana legislature was in session, and he asked him to use a medical publisher in order to minimize sensationalism. Kinsey chose W.B. Saunders, an old-line firm in Philadelphia. The original printing was slated for ten thousand but as prepublication interest grew, Saunders increased it to twenty-five thousand. The book cost $6.50, had 804 pages, and weighed three pounds. Kinsey had received no advance against royalties, and whatever money he made, he turned back to his own think tank, which by then was known as the Institute for Sex Research of Indiana University.

Though he continued to sign himself on letters "Alfred Kinsey, professor of zoology," his days as a mere professor were behind him. His name from then on was a household word; everyone knew of him as the sex doctor. Within ten days of the book's release the publisher had to order a sixth printing, making 185,000 copies in print, a remarkable number for so scholarly a piece of work. To the astonishment of everyone, particularly Kinsey, the book roared up the best-seller lists, a fact somewhat embarrassing to *The New York Times*, which at first neither accepted advertising for Kinsey's book nor reviewed it. The early critical response was good. The first reviews saw his samples adequate, his scientific judgments modest, his tone serious. Polls taken of ordinary Americans showed that not only did they agree with his evidence but they believed such studies were helpful.

Enduring Criticism

Then his critics weighed in. They furiously disagreed with almost everything: his figures on premarital sex, his figures on extramarital sex, his figures on homosexuality, and above all, his failure to condemn what he had found. Not only had he angered the traditional conservative bastions of social mores—the Protestant churches on the right, and the Catholic Church—but to his surprise he had enraged the most powerful voices in the liberal Protestant clergy as well. Henry Pitney Van Dusen, the head of Union Theological Seminary, and Reinhold Niebuhr attacked. Harry Emerson Fosdick, the head of [New York City's prestigious] Riverside Church and the brother of the head of the Rockefeller Foundation, complained that the advertising for the book was not sufficiently sedate. Harold Dodds, president of Princeton, said, "Perhaps the undergraduate newspaper that likened the report to the work of small boys writing dirty words on fences touched a more profound scientific truth than is revealed in the surfeit of rather trivial graphs with which the reports are loaded." By trying to study our sexual patterns, Kinsey was accused of trying to lower our moral standards.

Kinsey was at first stunned, then angered, but never embittered. He was appalled by the failure of other scientists and doctors to come to his defense, but what surprised him most was the absence of scientific standards in most of the assaults. His critics were, he noted, merely "exposing their emotional (not their scientific) selves in their attacks."

The attacks wounded Kinsey, yet he refused to show it in public. Besides, there was a second book to finish. His biggest fear was that he might lose his key source of support, the Rockefeller Foundation. Unfortunately Henry Pitney Van Dusen was not just the head of Union Theological; he was also a member of the Rockefeller Foundation board.

At first the foundation stood firm. Alan Gregg, who was in effect Kinsey's man at the foundation, congratulated Kinsey for handling himself so well in the face of such venomous criticism. But soon Gregg's tone began to change. He started suggesting that Kinsey show more statistical evidence in the next volume, and before long he was warning that it might be harder than he had expected to sustain the funding.

The trouble, Kinsey learned, was the new head of the Rockefeller Foundation, Dean Rusk. Rusk had come over after serving as the assistant secretary of state for Far Eastern affairs. Cautious to a fault, wary of the power of conservatives in Congress, he was not eager to take serious political risks on behalf of something that must have seemed as peripheral to him as sex research. B. Carroll Reece, a conservative Republican from Tennessee, was threatening to investigate the foundation, and one of the reasons was the Kinsey report. Kinsey sensed that Rusk was distancing himself from the institute.

Publishing the Second Report

The second book, *Sexual Behavior in the Human Female*, was published in the fall of 1953. Kinsey was well aware that it was even more explosive than the first; he was, after all, discussing wives, mothers, and daughters. As a precaution Kinsey invited journalists to come to Bloomington for several days so that he could explain the data to them and thereby help them interpret it.

Like the first book, it was a sensation. Within ten days the publishers were in their sixth printing; it would eventually sell some 250,000 copies. Again the initial reception was essentially positive; some of the magazine reporting was thoughtful. Then the fire storm began. "It is impossible to estimate the damage this book will do to the already deteriorating morals of America," [renowned evangelist] Billy Graham pronounced. The worst thing about the report, Van Dusen said, was not Kinsey's facts, if they were indeed trustworthy, but that they revealed "a prevailing degradation in American morality approximating the worst decadence of the Roman Empire. The most disturbing thing is the absence of spontaneous ethical revulsion from the premises of the study and the inability on the part of the readers to put their fingers on the falsity of its premises. For the presuppositions of the Kinsey Report are strictly animalistic. . . ." Again Kinsey was disheartened: "I am still uncertain what the basic reason for the bitter attack on us may be. The attack is evidently much more intense with this publication of the Female. Their arguments become absurd when they attempt to find specific flaws in the book and basically I think they are attacking on general principles."

Funding Denied

The new book was the final straw for the Rockefeller Foundation. In November 1953 Kinsey's supporters there made passionate presentations on his behalf and put in a request for eighty thousand dollars. Rusk rejected it. It was a shattering moment. Kinsey wrote a note to Rusk pleading with him to come out to Bloomington to see what they were doing and telling of how well things looked for the future. Later, in another letter to Rusk, he noted, "To have fifteen years of accumulated data in this area fail to reach publication would constitute an indictment of the Institute, its sponsors, and all others who have contributed time and material resources to the work."

Kinsey redoubled his efforts. If he had been driven before, now there was a manic quality to his work. His friends began to worry about his health. He suffered from insomnia, began to take sleeping pills, and started showing up groggy at work in the morning. Problems with his heart grew more serious. On several occasions he was hospitalized, and by the middle of 1956 he was forced to stay home and rest. In the summer of 1956 he conducted sex interviews number 7984 and 7985. On August 25, 1956, he died at the age of sixty-two.

Debating Women's Domestic Roles

Betty Friedan

Published in 1963 and recognized as a pivotal text in the women's movement, Betty Friedan's book The Feminine Mystique *created an intense debate over women's roles in the domestic sphere. The idea for the book was sparked by the results of a questionnaire Friedan handed out to her Smith College classmates at a fifteen-year reunion. Friedan condemned what she called the "feminine mystique," the prevailing cultural belief that women can only be fulfilled by becoming mothers and housewives. Because women are pressured to confine themselves to these narrow roles without the opportunity for education or career, they have difficulty developing their own identities, she contended. Before she expanded her research to a book-length project, three women's magazines refused to publish Friedan's work because it challenged conventional assumptions about femininity.*

In the following selection, Friedan shares and discusses some of the many letters she received from women after publishing The Feminine Mystique. *The responses to her criticism of the domestic female role range from heartfelt thanks to passionate resentment. This debate was an important stage in the sexual revolution. After publishing* The Feminine Mystique, *Friedan helped found the National Organization for Women in 1966. She subsequently also wrote* The Second Stage *(1981), in which she argues that feminists must reclaim the family and bring more men into the movement, and* The Fountain of Age *(1993), which addresses society's patronizing treatment of older citizens. She died in 2006.*

"Who am I? What shall I do with my own life?" These seem to be troubling questions for more and more American women, questions that have brought strongly worded responses in the hundreds of letters women have written to me from all over America since the publication of *The Feminine Mystique.*

Many were violently outraged at the charge that American women have been seduced back into the doll's house,[1] living through their husbands and children instead of finding individual identity in the modern world. As the proponent of this heresy, I was cursed, pitied, told to "get psychiatric help," to "go jump in the lake," and accused of being "more of a threat to the United States than the Russians."

Many correspondents suggested that American women would not be discontented in their "sacred role of housewife" if words like mine did not *make* them discontented.

But there were also hundreds of letters of another kind. A Florida mother of four: "I have been trying for years to tell my husband of my need to do something to find myself—to have a purpose. All I've ever achieved was to end up feeling guilty about wanting to be more than a housewife and mother." A woman from South Attleboro, Massachusetts: "I have for the past ten years now been asking myself, 'Is this all there is to life?' I am a housewife and mother of five children. I have a very poor education. I am thirty-eight years old, and if this is all there is for me to look forward to, I don't want to go on."

A twenty-six-year-old from Lansing, Michigan, whose three children are ready to begin their own lives: "Here I am! I feel like an appliance. I want to live! I want more education and a chance to compete in this world. My brain seems dead, and I am nothing but a parasite."

1. a reference to Henrik Ibsen's play *A Doll's House*

Trapped at Home

How often letters have come in, postmarked from small towns across the country, that have echoed and reechoed each other, as if a whole generation of women were humming together the same song of their lives.

From a small town in Georgia: "I had truly come to distrust anything I had read concerning women. None of it seemed to fit the picture of 'women' I had experienced by being a woman. My feelings are those of complete exhilaration.... You set up a challenge to me. I do not know that I have the strength or the perseverance to go through with it. I never thought of having a career, for I was not particularly bright.

"I felt I probably could not have really made the grade in a profession had I tried, so I considered marriage a career and tried to teach my children as much as they would allow me about the advanced thinking of the day. As they have reached teen-age they no longer listen but in fact rebuff whatever I may say. When my youngest starts to college I intend to go back too. So long as I can think of obtaining further education even if I never use it to earn money, the future seems exhilarating to me.... Otherwise, death pangs grip at my very being and a depression sets in that nearly drowns me."

Somehow, that either/or choice built into the feminine mystique seemed to doom women to contempt and self-contempt, loneliness, hostility, resentment whatever path they took....

Prejudice in the Job Market

But even women who were encouraged by their husbands in their efforts to find new paths faced implacable barriers, blocks, prejudices when they tried to go back to school or work. An Ivy League graduate described her interview with an alumnae vocational agency when she decided to look for a real job. "I asked what vocational opportunities were possible for a reasonably intelligent, energetic woman, holder of an A.B. degree. I was ready and willing to pursue future study or training, and I wanted some information about possibilities. I shall never forget the advice I received from the woman in charge of the agency, and I quote: 'Go back to your kitchen and stay there and make jam.' I was a sissy—I paid attention to her! I wonder how many other frustrated housewives have been similarly discouraged."

Many, it would seem—like this woman who tried to go back to her profession after the years of diapers and P.T.A. [parent-teacher association] meetings: "I was very happy doing it. My children have been honor students. Now they are almost grown and I am forty-five years old and find myself with time on my hands. Naturally I expected to go back into teaching. What a foolish dream! I was told that I was 'too old.' 'But,' I protested, 'there are women who are much older than I am teaching in schools all over town.' And back came the answer, 'Oh, but they have been teaching all these years. They don't have a twenty-year break in their teaching experience. A woman who has spent twenty years just being a housewife has nothing to contribute to the teaching profession.' Again I pleaded my cause: 'I am sure I have just as much to offer as the young girls just out of college.' 'No, that is not our point of view. The way we see it, the young girl is naïve and inexperienced. We can build her and shape her thinking the way we want it.'" . . .

Upholding the Domestic Role

Are there two distinctly different kinds of American women, or merely different *stages* in our growth as women? And if the latter is the case, isn't it possible for women at these different stages to help one another?

Even among these letters, I found that one woman's question became another woman's answer; one woman's answer, the question another woman had failed to ask . . .

Can a woman find herself by simply *being* "feminine," passive, and dependent on her husband? A California woman, who married at nineteen and quit college to stay home and have babies, wrote: "I happen to love the rewards of being completely passive, with just a hint of the aggressor at the right time. I don't want to compete with my husband. I want to respect and admire and love him. He's not working as hard as he is for himself. He's doing it all for me, for the same reason I'm keeping his house nice for him, cooking his meals, and being dependent on him. My whole life isn't *completely* centered around my home and family, but you can bet your bottom dollar ninety-five per cent of it is, and I love it. I'm sick of having my station in life referred to as trapped. Interview the young widow, and see if she wouldn't gladly call back the days she was 'submissive, dependent, and childlike, in her husband's shadow'!" . . .

Equal Roles in the Marriage

Are American men so weak that *they* cannot compete unless their wives dedicate themselves to help them—or is this a measure of a man's strength? A New York university graduate cum laude who worked her husband's way through graduate school found then that she could not "compete" herself in the field that interested her. Now she "chooses" to stay home and help her husband with *his* work.

"It is more important for me to have one worthwhile career involving both our efforts, than two mediocre ones," she writes. "I'm being coldly realistic about our capabilities. There's nothing wrong in a wife's pride in her husband's achievement if she has honestly been a part of it. It is difficult for men to retain pride and masculinity if the wife is more successful in her career."

But a woman who was divorced after twenty-three years as a "selfless housewife" writes: "While I was disturbed, it was also with an enormous sense of relief that I went back to college, got my M.A., and also found another husband. A man fosters the 'feminine mystique' because he can't tolerate a wife who is strong and independent. But if she habitually stays her hand and 'gives in' gracefully to his 'superior wisdom,' he is likely to know how phony he is—and they both wind up feeling that she is much brighter and more competent than she actually would be if forced to measure herself in reality against him, or alongside him. Men need to grow up enough to be able to act independently without the constant validation of somebody weaker. So do women. If they can't, they'll either encourage a 'child-husband' or have child after child."

Debating the Nature of Womanhood

What is real womanhood? "Real women are loved, needed, wanted, and desired because we are happy, having learned the finest lesson of all: selflessness," says one woman. And an unhappy echo comes from another: "It takes a real woman to sit home every night raising his kids while he's living it up high, wide and handsome in a nice clean shirt she washed and ironed and starched for him, so some other woman could smear lipstick all over it. I am fighting for a man I have always loved and always will."

The mother who considers femininity her "blessing" from God may have a daughter who curses its name. "Being a good housewife and mother is a most fulfilling role which God planned for all womankind and for which He especially equipped her with such assets as the ability to be all-loving, self-sacrificing, gentle, feminine," says a New Jersey housewife. "It is reward enough for me to see my husband busy but happy, my children leaders in their schools, because I am at home each day making beds, cooking good meals, and ready to listen with a full heart and ear to problems, sorrows, and joys." . . .

The Ethical Choice

"The real answer would seem to be for today's women not to

produce children," says a letter from Anaheim, California, bit-terly. "That way they could write, paint, compete with men in the world of business, work side by side with the scientists, participate in politics, and express themselves all over the place."

How many women—and children, marriages and talents—have been maimed by the perpetuation of that either/or choice? One woman, in Eau Gallie, Florida, developed a recur-rent toxic condition which required surgery rendering her sterile. Her relationship with her husband deteriorated; her gifted oldest child developed personality problems; and she fi-nally became so "tired, listless, and bored with the humdrum routine that books were too much effort to get through, and even my house was beginning to look neglected." Finally she broke away, went back to school, "and came alive again." . . .

An Alternative

How ingenious an American woman can be when she really wants to! An Illinois mother of six does her shopping early, picks up her baby-sitter, and retypes the paper she wrote at midnight before her first class at the University of Illinois at 12:30. Her youngest child is just a year old, her oldest child nine, and she is graduating this summer with honors and a degree in elementary education.

"Most of my neighbors think I'm crazy. Nevertheless, I doubt that many women are as happy as I. The children ac-cept the fact that I have a life of my own. There are scholar-ships and loans; I have both in sufficient amounts to take care of baby-sitting expenses. All that is really needed is a husband who sees his wife as a real person in her own right." . . .

From a woman in Iowa whose education stopped at high school: "Thank God someone had the insight and courage to write it. It struck at the center of my being. I am finally confi-dent of myself and my desire to launch the career I've wanted for so long. The last of the cobwebs of guilt have been swept away, and what a marvelous free feeling! The release of women from this subtle bondage can only be good and right. How can it help but add a new dimension to the lives of the male as well as the female, even if it might be unwelcome by the male at first. How great the responsibility to be the superior sex. How it must weigh on those who prove inadequate to live up to the myth. I have been able now to rid myself of the resentment I have felt towards my husband in particular and men in general. I am on the threshold of a new life. I feel alive and excited for the first time in years."

LIVING THROUGH
THE COLD WAR

CHAPTER 2

Changes in Sexual Values

Advocating Sexual Freedom

David Allyn

In the following selection David Allyn describes the emergence of the Sexual Freedom League (SFL) in the 1960s. The league was originally formed in New York City to promote the idea of sexual freedom and to oppose the prevailing conservative sexual values. Later in the decade, the SFL expanded into a network of chapters across the country. Allyn focuses on the founding members of the SFL in order to illustrate how the organization's rise both reflected and shaped the changing sexual norms of the time. The SFL specifically opposed laws restricting nudity, the availability of contraception, and unconventional sexual practices. Allyn received his PhD from Harvard University and has taught history at Princeton University. His articles appear in the Washington Post, *the* Boston Globe, *the* New York Daily News, *and the* Journal of American Studies.

August is a cold month in San Francisco. The city has its real summer in September and October. But in August 1965, two young men and two young women tentatively stripped off their clothes and staged a nude "wade-in" off a San Francisco city beach. Imitating civil rights protesters in the South, the four self-proclaimed sexual-freedom fighters disobeyed local laws and customs to make a point about personal liberty. Jefferson Poland, the twenty-three-year-old leader of the group, believed anti-nudity ordinances were a denial of basic civil liberties and, worse, led to sexual repression in society. The founder of the New York League for Sexual Freedom, which by 1965 had evolved into the "national" Sexual Freedom League, Jeff Poland knew that a nude wade-in would capture the attention of the media. He forgot that in August, temperatures in San Francisco often dipped below 60 degrees.

The week before the protest, he organized a handful of supporters, mostly North Beach beatniks, and alerted the local press. On the morning of the appointed day, Poland, wearing a swimsuit and a flower behind his ear, arrived with his three friends at the municipal beach known as Aquatic Park. Before cheering crowds and several cameramen, the four would-be protesters entered the icy ocean water and three of them disrobed (the fourth got scared at the last minute). A nineteen-year-old anarchist supporter stood on the shore and waved a banner asking, "Why Be Ashamed Of Your Body?" Other supporters formed a picket line on the beach and chanted, "Sex is clean! Law's obscene!" Reporters, unimpressed with the skinny-dipping stunt but eager for a good story, urged the nude swimmers to return to the shore in order to get arrested. Soon enough they were cited for violating San Francisco's municipal code regulating swimming attire. The two women received suspended sentences and six months' probation. Poland was required to spend five weekends in jail. (It was well known at the time that President [Lyndon B.] Johnson liked to swim naked in the White House pool, a fact that some members of the press thought was indicative of a certain hypocrisy on the part of public officials.) The story made the national news.

Jefferson Poland

Jefferson Poland was one of the first hippies. He was wearing flowers in his hair well before the rest of his generation. He was a beatnik who, several years before it would become a trend, dropped the pretensions of urbane ultrasophistication for the back-to-nature simplicity of Rousseauian[1] romanticism, a long-haired kid who saw the power of combining utopian social protest with over-the-top theatrics while the majority of male college students were still wearing jackets and ties to class.

---

1. Jean-Jacques Rousseau was a Swiss philosopher who believed the individual was essentially good but was usually corrupted by society.

44

Born in Indiana in 1942, just before the beginning of the postwar baby boom, Poland was the son of working-class parents. His father was a machinist in an automobile manufacturing plant, his mother a pink-collar worker [one who works in jobs traditionally held by women]. As a boy he often wet his bed. His father, determined to "cure" him of this habit, would come into his bedroom every morning and check to see if the bed was wet. If it was, he would tell Jeff to strip and then whipped the naked boy with a belt. Eventually Jeff told his mother about his father's beatings, and mother and son fled to Houston, Texas. They remained on the move. Jefferson attended over twenty schools before going to college. As a result, he perpetually felt like a "newcomer," an exceptionally creative outsider who "retreated into books" and "hardly knew anyone except" his mother.

Jefferson eventually left his mother's home and began hitchhiking his way to California. On one occasion he had sex with a man who gave him a ride; he enjoyed the experience, but also felt an intense sense of shame. He became an itinerant student, drifting in and out of schools, searching for meaning and purpose. By the time he was eighteen, he was having sex with women. He began to question sexual mores, and as an undergraduate at San Francisco State University turned to popular authors like Philip Wylie and Albert Ellis to make sense of his own sexual tastes and the assumptions of American society. Their texts piqued Poland's interest in erotic freedom, but he felt frustrated by the fact that "sexual liberation seemed to exist mainly in books."

Hearing About Free Love

Like other young beatniks, Poland moved into a group house to save rent. His roommates were two young women, both of them self-proclaimed anarchists. They taught Poland about "free love," a doctrine of anarchism since the movement began in the early 1900s. Such prominent anarchists as Emma Goldman and her lover Ben Reitman had criticized monogamous marriage as a form of property ownership in numerous articles and public speeches. (In her personal life, Goldman had tried to live according to her beliefs but was consumed with jealousy when Reitman had relationships with other women.) Free love was trumpeted even earlier by Victoria Woodhull, a radical suffragist who, in the 1870s, had several husbands and numerous lovers. By the 1960s, anarchism was all but dead in America, but the idea that monogamy and jealousy were outdated and ought to be abolished had survived among intellectuals and bohemians. Poland was quickly converted to the cause.

Many of the left-wing dissidents of the early sixties congregated at Poland's group house. One was former University of Illinois biology professor Leo Koch, who was famous among radicals for being fired from his teaching position because of a letter he'd written to the student newspaper in defense of premarital sex. Koch had tried to sue the university and, having lost in the lower courts, was still awaiting a decision by the Supreme Court.

Poland, deeply impressed by Koch's sense of conviction and willingness to challenge moral authority, decided to dedicate himself to the cause of sexual freedom. When comedian Lenny Bruce was arrested on obscenity charges in San Francisco in 1961, Poland participated in protests on Bruce's behalf. At San Francisco State, Poland ran for student office on a platform promising the sale of contraceptives in the school bookstore. Poland lost the election but not his interest in politics.

Forming the League

In the summer of 1963, Poland, like hundreds of other college students, joined the civil rights movement as a volunteer. He endured the summer heat to register voters in Louisiana, where he learned about the growing student movement. In the fall, he moved to New York City in search of work. Two days after the assassination of John F. Kennedy in November 1963, Poland again met Leo Koch. Koch was well connected in Manhattan, and he introduced Poland to the writers of the New York Beat scene. Poland met Allen Ginsberg [author of the influential poem "Howl"], who had returned to New York after several years in San Francisco; Diane Di Prima, one of the few women in the Beat community of poets; Ed Sanders, editor of a Beat journal named . . . *You: A Magazine of the Arts;* and Tuli Kupferberg, a pacifist and songwriter. Poland also met avant-garde actors, directors, and playwrights like Judith Malina and Julian Beck, the founders of the Living Theater, an experimental troupe that used nudity to challenge conventional morality.

In January 1964, the Supreme Court announced that it would not review Koch's case against the University of Illinois. In response, Poland and Koch decided to form a group to challenge American sexual laws and values. They took the name the League for Sexual Freedom, mistakenly believing it to have been the name of an earlier organization formed in Germany (the organization they probably had in mind was the World League for Sexual Reform founded in 1928 by sexual scientist Magnus Hirschfeld). Such literary luminaries as Beck, Ginsberg, Di Prima, Sanders, Peter Orlovsky, and Paul Krassner were founding members. But Poland, Kupferberg, and a young activist named Randy Wicker were the real leaders of the League.

Tuli Kupferberg

Tuli Kupferberg, a so-called "red diaper baby" because he was the son of Communist Party members, was an anarchist and a sexual radical in his own right. Like other anarchists, Kupferberg rejected monogamy as an outdated, bourgeois notion. He and his wife had an agreement that both were free to sleep with other people. In the mid-sixties, he and Ed Sanders formed a folk-rock band, the Fugs, named after Norman Mailer's euphemism in his war novel *The Naked and the Dead* (1948). Their songs were silly yet provocative, with titles like "Group Grope," "Boobs a Lot," "Kill for Peace," "What Are You Doing After the Orgy?," and "Dirty Old Man." The Fugs appealed to fellow bohemians and the growing number of baby boomers who were seeking alternatives to the sappy lyrics and melodies of pop music.

As soon as Kupferberg and Poland met, they became close friends, sharing as they did an interest in sexual freedom. Kupferberg was a devotee of Wilhelm Reich, the renegade psychoanalyst who believed that sex and politics were deeply linked. Reich had been one of [the founder of psychoanalysis, Sigmund] Freud's leading disciples during the early years of psychoanalysis; unlike Freud, however, Reich was a socialist who thought it imperative to combine political activism and sexual theory. Sexual repression, Reich argued, was the cornerstone of totalitarianism, so in order to liberate people politically it was necessary to liberate them sexually first. But Reich was eventually expelled from the Communist Party, rejected by Freud, and ultimately forced into exile by the Nazis. In 1939, he fled to the United States, where he acquired a small but influential group of followers, all of whom subscribed to his notion that sexual repression caused serious psychological damage. In line with his teachings, Reichian analysts taught their patients how to achieve maximum pleasure through intercourse and thereby experience the full release of all pent-up energies. Reich died in 1957 and his library was destroyed by the federal government, but thirty-one Reichian analysts continued to practice his techniques, and his ideas infused the writings of many important intellectuals of the sixties. Kupferberg spent time in Reichian therapy, and Reich's ideas underscored Kupferberg's own beliefs about sexual freedom.

Another Important Matter

Randy Wicker, the third leading figure in the Sexual Freedom League, was no stranger to sexual politics when he met Jefferson Poland and Tuli Kupferberg in the early sixties. Wicker had been involved for several years with the Mattachine Society, the gay rights organization founded in the fifties in New York by Rudi Gernreich and his friend Harry Hay. In 1962, Wicker had successfully persuaded a New York radio station to allow gay men to speak on the air about their own lives, a first for American radio. In addition, he convinced reporters to write stories on homosexual life for the *Village Voice,* the *New York Post,* and *Harpers.* But when a female friend needed an abortion and could not find a doctor willing to perform the operation (she ended up taking quinine, having a miscarriage, and spending several years in Bellevue mental hospital), Wicker realized that sexual freedom meant more than gay rights. Like Kupferberg, Wicker became a founding member of the New York League for Sexual Freedom in 1964.

At first, the New York League members merely engaged in discussion. At weekly gatherings in Greenwich Village, Poland, Kupferberg, Wicker, and others would meet to debate the meaning of "sexual freedom." The discussions often dwelled on hypothetical situations, lending an abstract, intellectual dimension to the organization's endeavor. They argued the moral merits of prostitution, pedophilia, bestiality (the group decided bestiality was okay if an animal failed to resist), and other controversial sex practices. Wicker recalls that one of the liveliest discussions involved the legitimacy of public masturbation. The group members decided that there was nothing wrong with it so long as a man did not actually hit someone with his semen during ejaculation, which would be a violation of the other person's rights. There were fewer than a dozen core members of the group, but every so often prominent figures in New York's avant-garde would join in the discussions.

Protesting for Change

Occasionally, group members would stand on the streets of Manhattan and pass out fliers about sexual freedom. To jaded urban passersby, League members were a mere curiosity. In April 1964, League members held a speak-out at Columbia University, hoping that college students would rally to their cause. Poland and his fellow activists demanded "respect for sexual freedom as a fundamental civil liberty," and called for the decriminalization of interracial marriage, fellatio, cunnilingus, anal intercourse, bestiality, and transvestism. They also attacked censorship laws, laws against public nudity, laws against contraception and abortion, college parietal rules [rules governing the visiting privileges of members of the opposite sex in college dorms], statutory rape laws, and strict divorce laws. They called for the freedom of "homosexuals and other harmless deviates" from police persecution and for the legalization of prostitution "under conditions which will reduce VD [venereal disease] and protect the welfare of prostitutes."

League members were as concerned about sexual equality as they were about sexual freedom. "Each person," they announced, "should be free to choose his or her activities and roles without being forced by social pressure or law to conform to rigid masculine and feminine stereotypes."

A Series of Demonstrations

Taking their cue from the burgeoning civil rights movement, the League members staged a series of demonstrations, some more successful than others. An early protest targeted the New York City district attorney's office after city police arrested filmmaker Jonas Mekas in March 1964 on obscenity charges for showing an underground film called *Flaming Creatures*, which contained close-up images of breasts and genitals, men in drag, and suggestions of masturbation, oral sex, and gang rape. Then when comedian Lenny Bruce was again arrested on obscenity charges in April, Allen Ginsberg and other members of the League organized a committee to fight for his release. Ginsberg issued a press release with the signatures of dozens of important intellectuals. The League also organized a protest in front of the New York Public Library in an effort to bring attention to the library's policy of segregating sex books. On August 23, 1964, the League sponsored a demonstration outside the Women's House of Detention, where a majority of inmates were prostitutes. Jeff Poland, who picketed in front of the building carrying an American flag, attracted the attention of some reporters by calling for the total decriminalization of prostitution. Then, on September 19, Poland and Wicker sponsored the first public demonstration for homosexual rights in New York City. Together they protested the military's policy of investigating and outing "suspected homosexuals" by picketing the city's Armed Forces Induction Center. In October, when Walter Jenkins, an assistant to Lyndon Johnson, was forced to resign over allegations of engaging in homosexual activity in a public rest room, the League adopted a statement in his defense. League members also organized public education sessions at Albert Ellis's Institute for Rational Emotive Therapy. But none of these activities attracted much public notice or galvanized a genuine political movement. . . .

When Poland arrived in San Francisco in the spring of 1965, students at UC Berkeley were embroiled in a controversy over the politics of profanity. The "filthy speech movement" (so called because it grew out of the "Free Speech movement," which had involved a series of campus protests a few months earlier against university rules about political activism on university property) was forcing nearly everyone in California to reexamine their views about morality and censorship. . . .

The League Gains Momentum

Jefferson Poland was not directly involved in the filthy speech movement, but he was certainly inspired by the publicity it generated. In August 1965, as the filthy speech controversy finally dissipated, Poland organized the nude wade-in, thereby taking the entire issue of candor one step further. Like generations of nudists before him, Poland believed that there was nothing obscene about the naked body. Laws against nakedness, Poland felt, produced unhealthy attitudes and a cultural obsession with sex. According to the Bible, nudists pointed out, God ordered Isaiah to go naked for three years, while King David danced naked in the town square.

Newspaper and magazine reports of his August wade-in gave Poland a national spotlight. He renamed his group, calling it the Sexual Freedom League (as opposed to the New York League for Sexual Freedom), and invited interested members across the country to form regional chapters.

Student Activism

By now college campuses were bulging with baby boomers. Student populations were larger than they had ever been. These young people knew about the pill; they had read *Playboy* and Helen Gurley Brown [author of the controversial *Sex and the Single Girl*] in high school. As one sex educator wrote approvingly, "A very real freedom now exists for adolescent couples and for youth in mixed groups to speak openly and frankly about sexual matters." Like Poland many of them had no patience with their parents' hypocrisy: their willingness, for instance, to accept nudity in a titillating magazine like *Playboy* but not on the beaches of San Francisco. Within a year after the wade-in, sexual freedom groups had formed at Stanford, UC Berkeley, UCLA, and the University of Texas. Stanford's Sexual Freedom Forum issued a Statement of Principles, which read: "We view sexual rights as a proper extension of individual civil liberties. We prefer open honest acceptance of varying personal sexual practices to the massive hypocrisy of many parts of our society. . . . The private sexual activities of consenting adults are sacrosanct." A photo in the *San Francisco Chronicle* showed a handsome young man and two attractive "coeds" handing out leaflets on the college campus. The members of the Stanford Sexual Freedom Forum managed to collect 450 student signatures supporting the distribution of contraception to unmarried women. Students then voted in favor of the measure, 1,866 to 853. The director of Stanford's health service derided the Forum's efforts as "a tragically crude and simplistic approach to an enormously complex and sensitive issue." But as students began selling buttons with the slogan "Make Love, Not War," the link between sexual freedom and student activism was cemented. The slogan expressed the commonly held view that sexual liberation would lead to a decrease in social tensions. "Our capacity for violence," wrote Jefferson Poland and Sam Sloan in *The Sex Marchers*, "is a spill-over, a natural consequence of our repressed sexuality, our caged libidos." As a pithy response to the escalating war in Vietnam, the slogan quickly captured the media's attention.

Working for Change

At the University of Texas in Austin, the Student League for Responsible Sexual Freedom counted fifteen members in 1966, who opposed limiting the sale of contraceptives on campus to married women and sought the decriminalization of homosexuality and the repeal of laws against sodomy. Texas state senator Grady Hazelwood threatened that he would "never vote another appropriation for the University" if the group were not abolished. The day after Hazelwood's threat, the university banned the group from campus. At Merritt Junior College in Oakland, where Jefferson Poland was now enrolled, the Merritt Sexual Freedom Forum, following the lead of their peers at Stanford, succeeded in putting the distribution of birth control on the school ballot in the spring of 1966. Across the country, Sexual Freedom League chapters took on a variety of issues. At the University of Florida, the school chapter of the Sexual Freedom League vocally opposed miscegenation laws. Members of the Berkeley Campus Sexual Freedom Forum were inspired by this effort and in November 1966 declared in their Resolution on Race and Gender as Sexual Re strictions "each of us must make special efforts to overcome these barriers and find lovers of different races." As the Sexual Freedom League grew, so did the idea that a sexually liberated society would be less exploitative, less tempted by mass-market pornography, suggestive advertising, and other forms of commercialized titillation. When a representative of *Playboy* came to Iowa's Grinnell College to speak in 1965, students, male and female, protested what they perceived as *Playboy*'s pseudo-liberated philosophy by coming to the talk naked. . . .

Don't Ask, Don't Tell

Premarital sex was a fact on college campuses, and administrators knew they could never punish one student for having sex without punishing hundreds, if not thousands. As a Yale University dean told a reporter in 1966, "We are not interested in the private lives of students as long as they remain private." Ruth Darling, an assistant dean at Cornell, agreed: "We don't ask what they do and don't want to know." In 1965, the Group for the Advancement of Psychiatry, representing 260 psychiatrists, published a report on parietal rules and campus sexual behavior. The report, *Sex and the College Student,* advised administrators to ignore private sexual behavior. "The student's privacy requires respect; sexual activity privately practiced with appropriate attention to the sensitivities of other people should not be the direct concern of the administration." Though controversial, the report had a strong influence on academics and administrators.

Following this advice from the psychiatric experts, college administrators in the mid-sixties essentially adopted a "don't ask, don't tell" policy on premarital sex. But such a policy could work only if students agreed to draw a sharp line between their private and public lives, keeping their sexual activity secret. The members of the Sexual Freedom League had already shown their unwillingness to pretend that sex was purely a private matter. So long as there were laws regulating speech, dress, and consensual sexual behavior, sex would never be purely private. As far as Sexual Freedom League members were concerned, they were not making sex public, they were merely acknowledging its already public dimension. . . .

By the beginning of 1966, Jefferson Poland had faded from the national scene. He remained a colorful figure in the Bay Area counterculture . . . , but the increasingly dramatic events of the sixties overshadowed Poland's modest efforts to effect social change. Across the country, thousands of students joined protests against the Vietnam War and thousands more let their hair grow long and began calling themselves "freaks," and later, "hippies." Just as Poland had tucked a flower behind his ear when he stripped in San Francisco's Aquatic Park, hippies worshiped flowers as symbols of peace. They also staged playful stunts to disrupt the daily routines of the somnambulant middle class. As the ranks of the hippies grew, Jefferson Poland and his fellow Sexual Freedom Leaguers believed bourgeois morality to be on the brink of collapse. The gates of Eden were to be reopened at last.

Social Changes Brought by the Pill

Elizabeth Siegel Watkins

The U.S. Food and Drug Administration approved the sale of the birth control pill in 1960. Many argue that no other drug in history has had as great an effect on American culture. This highly convenient form of birth control made it much easier for women to have sex with almost no risk of becoming pregnant. This development allowed women to be more sexually liberated and to more easily put off childbearing in order to pursue careers. In addition, the pill created a more open attitude toward sex and added fuel to the feminist and pro-choice movements.

Included in the key group of people to bring about the invention of the pill were Margaret Sanger and Katharine McCormick, two elderly women who wanted a form of birth control that would be as easy to use as taking an aspirin. Sanger and McCormick provided the initial funding for research in the 1950s. John Rock, an obstetrician and gynecologist at Harvard University and also a member of the Catholic Church, became the unofficial spokesperson for the drug he believed allowed Catholics a full and healthy sex life. Though there was intense debate among Catholics, Pope Paul VI ultimately stated (in 1968) that the church remained opposed to all forms of birth control except the rhythm method (based on a women's fertility cycle). Two years after the pope's decision it was revealed that two-thirds of Catholic women were using contraceptives—28 percent of them the pill. A final key player was Gregory Pincus, a talented biologist who persuaded the pharmaceutical company Searle to market the drug despite tremendous risks.

After its introduction, use of the pill accelerated dramatically, from 1.2 million women in 1962 to 6.5 million in 1965 to 12.5

Elizabeth Siegel Watkins, *On the Pill: A Social History of Oral Contraceptives, 1950–1970.* Baltimore: Johns Hopkins University Press, 1998. Copyright © 1998 by Johns Hopkins University Press. Reproduced by permission.

million worldwide in 1967. Because the use of the pill was so widespread, its effects on society and culture were significant but complex. Elizabeth Siegel Watkins, in the following excerpt from her book On the Pill, *attempts to sort out some of the social implications of the pill for Americans during the sexual revolution. She contends that from the time of its arrival, the pill has been equated with the sexual revolution among the general public. Many women have welcomed the freedom the pill affords while critics have condemned the pill for eroding sexual morality. Watkins teaches at the University of California at San Francisco and is currently studying the history of estrogen replacement theory.*

Retrospective accounts of the 1960s often cite the pill as one of the causes of the sexual revolution. One researcher [Linda Grant], for example, pointed out that the best alternative to the pill, the diaphragm, never achieved great popularity; while tolerable within the confines of marriage, it was "less suitable for the one-night stand." She doubted that the sexual revolution would have happened without the pill. Other writers took the opposing view. They argued for sociological rather than technological causes of the sexual revolution, and dismissed the pill as either a necessary or sufficient antecedent.

The Convenience of the Pill

Of all the available methods of birth control that separated sexual intercourse from reproduction, the oral contraceptive prevented pregnancy most effectively. Women appreciated this reliability as well as the independence of this method from sexual intercourse. Perhaps the complete separation of contraception from intercourse was the pill's most innovative quality; women took their daily pills at a time and place unrelated to the act of coitus. Oral contraception was neither messy nor interruptive. Many women found swallowing a small tablet once a day for twenty days each month to be more appealing than fumbling with a diaphragm and jelly or persuading their partners to wear a condom. As Margaret Sanger had argued, women also preferred the pill because they controlled the method of birth control. A woman did not need the consent of her sexual partner to take the pill to prevent conception. Although later in the decade some feminists would become disillusioned with the pretense of sexual freedom, in the 1960s the pill offered many women the opportunity to enjoy sex with whomever they pleased without the fear of getting pregnant.

The aesthetic quality of the pill also helped to sanitize and to popularize sex. Its sobriquet, "the pill," offered a neutral term with which one could talk about birth control and by implication sexual intercourse. The acceptability of discussing sex in public paralleled the new openness regarding sexual matters in books, movies, advertising, and other aspects of popular culture. Magazines quickly heralded the new sexual revolution and speculated about its effects on society. For those who did not participate personally, media coverage provided the next best thing to being there. As Blanche Linden-Ward and Carol Hurd Green commented in their book, *American Women in the 1960s,* "Americans perceived social change as happening at a rapid and dangerous pace, while for the great majority, change came slowly if at all. Increased access to the news and pressure on news sources to fill their pages and broadcast hours meant that most Americans saw and heard much more than they experienced." For example, *Time* illustrated a cover story in 1964 about "The Second Sexual Revolution" with photos of pornographic magazines, women in skimpy bikinis, and couples making out in public. Such images could easily convince readers that the old rules governing sex and morality no longer applied in American society.

A Symbol of the Sexual Revolution

During the 1960s, journalists watched the innovation of oral contraception closely to determine its effects on sexual morality and activity. As time went on, they adopted the pill as the emblem of the sexual revolution. What is interesting about this representation is the implied relationship between the availability of the birth control pill and the shift toward more liberal sexual ethics. Articles in the popular media contributed to this association by speculating on the moral and social ramifications of easily obtainable, highly effective oral contraception. However, no data existed to confirm this hypothesis because no sociological research was undertaken in the 1960s to assess this relationship. Sociologists studied the incidence of premarital sex among college students, but did not correlate this activity with use of the pill (or any other contraceptive method). Demographic studies of the use of birth control included only married women; the first study of contraceptive use among unmarried teenagers was not conducted until the early 1970s. Researchers in sexology and family planning engaged in completely unrelated activities, producing noncomplementary data. The pill did indeed revolutionize birth control, and radical changes in sexual attitudes and conduct did take place, particularly among young people, but no one ever established a connection between these two phenomena.

Nonetheless, iconography and imagery of the pill as a symbol of the sexual revolution took hold and endured. In 1969, *Playboy* printed a cartoon of a beaming bride asking her new husband as they drove away from the church, "Can I stop taking the pill now?" Whether or not the pill contributed to increased sexual activity among the unmarried youth of America, popular magazines fostered the perception of its link with liberalized sexual conduct, and this perception developed into a lasting impression. At the time, the pill figured prominently in discussions of changing sexual morality; thirty years later, the correlation between the availability of oral contraception and the sexual revolution persists. Demographic, sociological, and popular treatments of the pill, sex, and morality in the 1960s provide clues to the construction of the link between oral contraception and the sexual revolution.

Misconceptions

Two important contradictions muddled contemporary evaluations of the pill. First, while the public generally accepted oral contraception as a superior form of fertility control, the use of the pill outside of marriage caused consternation among those who would preserve the sexual status quo. The conflation of the contraceptive revolution with the sexual revolution led many people to view the pill as "part of the problem" of sexual liberation among America's youth. Second, the proscription against use of the pill (or any other method of birth control) by unmarried women was generally limited to the middle and upper classes. On the other hand, birth control was recommended for poor women, both single and married, particularly those on welfare. These advocates considered the pill to be "part of the solution" to overpopulation.

Black Opposition

However, not everyone agreed that birth control for the purpose of population control was beneficial. Some militant blacks portrayed the pill as a genocidal weapon, and they accused white population controllers of trying to diminish the black race in America. A minority of black men saw the birth control pill as another example of white coercion of blacks and fostered the image of the pill as a racist tool. Black women, on the other hand, rejected the notion of genocide as absurd. When a mobile Planned Parenthood clinic in Pittsburgh closed after the leader of a militant group accused Planned Parenthood of discriminatory tactics and threatened to firebomb the office, the women in the community organized to seek the return of the clinic to their neighborhood. They resented the self-appointed spokesman for black Pittsburghers and argued that the use of birth control was a woman's personal decision. Within parts of the black community, evaluations of the pill broke down along gender lines. For these women, as for so many other women around the country, the pill represented a measure of freedom: to choose how many children to have, if any at all, and when to have them.

These conflicting perceptions of the role and significance of the pill were colored by undertones of classism, racism, and gender bias. Concerns about the safety of the pill superseded consideration of its moral and political consequence in the late 1960s, but at mid-decade the public focused its attention squarely on the pill as an element of social change.

The Impact of
Playboy Magazine

Deborah G. Felder

In 1953 Hugh Hefner, believing that men were becoming more receptive to sexual permissiveness, created a men's magazine featuring nude photographs along with general articles like those found in mainstream magazines. The publication sold well immediately. By the 1960s Playboy *had become an icon for a new openness to sexuality. The magazine even began to represent a particular masculine lifestyle of overt sexuality and sophistication, the "Playboy lifestyle." From its inception to its current publication, many people have criticized the magazine for objectifying women.*

In this selection, Deborah G. Felder relates the history and mission of the magazine while also highlighting the larger effects Playboy *had on American culture. She pays particular attention to feminist criticism of the magazine. Felder is the author of* The 100 Most Influential Women of All Time: A Ranking of Past and Present, Fifty Jewish Women Who Changed the World, *and* A Bookshelf of Our Own: Works That Changed Women's Lives, *in addition to other works.*

In retrospect, *Playboy*'s creator, Hugh Hefner, has repeatedly interpreted the launching of his magazine as an ideological assault on America's Puritan ethic of repressed sexuality and hypocritical morality, concepts that had been recently exposed by the revelations in Alfred Kinsey's *Sexual Behavior in the Human Male* (1948) and *Sexual Behavior in the Human Female* (1953). As Hefner explains, "I was trying to put out a magazine for myself, one that I would enjoy reading. It described an urban world and the play and pleasure parts of life. If you had to sum up the idea of *Playboy,* it is anti-Puritanism. Not just in regard to sex, but the whole range of play and pleasure." With the loosening of sexual mores and the increasing affluence of postwar American life, Hefner conceived of a magazine to celebrate both. As Hefner says, *"Playboy* came along and offered a new set of ethical values for the urban society. The editorial message in *Playboy* came through loud and clear: Enjoy yourself. Paul Gebhard, director of the Institute for Sex Research, once said that the genius of *Playboy* was that it linked sex with upward mobility, and that's a sociological way of expressing what I'm talking about."

Playboy Gets Its Start

The facts surrounding the creation of *Playboy* both support Hefner's contentions and qualify them with more practical, commercial considerations. Hefner, born in 1926, raised by strict Methodist parents, was a shy introvert desperate to enjoy the good life he felt excluded from in a series of low-level editorial jobs in Chicago following his discharge from the army and graduation from the University of Illinois in Urbana. A less than accomplished cartoonist and occasional satirist of the Chicago scene, with almost no money or experience, Hefner set out to launch his own men's magazine to achieve success and the liberation he had longed for at home, in the army, at school, and in his faltering marriage. As he remembers, "The most popular men's magazines of the time were the outdoor-adventure books—*True, Argosy,* and the like. They had a hairy-chested editorial emphasis with articles on hunting, fishing, chasing the Abominable Snowman over Tibetan mountaintops. . . . *Esquire* had changed its editorial emphasis after the war, eliminating most of the lighter material— the girls, cartoons, and humor. So the field was wide open for the sort of magazine I had in mind." To fill the void left by *Esquire* in the area of sophisticated male entertainment, Hefner planned his magazine, originally called *Stag Party,* with a philosophy that he announced in the first issue, published in December 1953:

> If you are a man between 18 and 80, *Playboy* is meant for you. . . . We want to make clear from the very start, we aren't a "family magazine." If you're somebody's sister, wife, or mother-in-law and picked us up by mistake, please pass us along to the man in your life and get back to *Ladies' Home Companion.* Within the pages of *Playboy* you will find articles, fiction, picture stories, cartoons, humor and special features culled from many sources, past and present, to form a pleasure-primer styled to the masculine taste.
>
> Most of today's "magazines for men" spend all their time out-of-doors—thrashing through thorny thickets or splashing about in fast-flowing streams. We'll be out there too, occasionally, but we don't mind telling you in advance—we plan spending most of our time inside.
>
> We like our apartment. We enjoy mixing up cocktails and an *hors d'oeuvre* or two, putting a little mood music on the phonograph and inviting in a female acquaintance for a quiet discussion of Picasso, Nietzsche, jazz, sex. . . .
>
> Affairs of the state will be out of our province. We don't expect to solve any world problems or prove any great moral truths. If we are able to give the American male a few extra laughs and a little diversion from the anxieties of the Atomic Age, we'll feel we've justified our existence.

Sex Sells

To create a sensation for his new magazine, Hefner fortuitously acquired the rights from a Chicago-based calendar printer of nude photographs of a young Marilyn Monroe taken in 1949 to help her pay the rent before she became a star. For the first time in American publishing, a mainstream magazine published full-color nude photographs, and the conjunction of the *Playboy* philosophy and the sensation of seeing a nude Hollywood goddess brought Hefner immediate and overwhelming success. Instantly profitable, *Playboy*'s circulation grew from 53,991 for the first issue to 2 million copies a month in 1964 to its height in 1972 of 7 million copies, earning profits of $12 million for the year.

Although *Playboy* eventually published first-rate fiction and articles by important writers and journalists and featured a series of interviews with important figures, its depiction of sex continued to define the magazine and ensure its phenomenal success. Prior to *Playboy*, nudity in magazines was occasional, confined to such publications as *Modern Sunbathing* and cheap girlie magazines. Hefner's Playmates, selected because they were not professional models but "girls next door," posed in recognizable settings, the opposite of the studio shots and the "rather self-conscious fallen look . . . like the girls in other girlie magazines." *Playboy*'s first new-style Playmate was Charlaine Karalus, who worked for the magazine. She appeared in 1955, named "Janet Pilgrim," along with this editorial comment: "We suppose that it's natural to think of the pulchritudinous Playmates as existing in a world apart. Actually, potential Playmates are all around you: the new secretary at your office, the doe-eyed beauty who sat opposite you at lunch yesterday, the girl who sells your shirts and ties in your favorite store. We found Miss July in our own circulation department, processing subscriptions. . . ." Hefner had freed nudity from its former shadowy world of the professional and cultist to feature ordinary women willing to appear *déshabillé* [undressed] in a national magazine. But the "average-looking," wholesome Playmates were enhanced to airbrushed perfection, with every blemish or flaw carefully removed by body makeup or retouches. Pubic hair was banned until 1971. The overall effect achieved a perfectibility of a woman's body in the terms that defined the magazine's notion of sensuality: statuesque, perfectly proportioned, and slightly vapid, a kind of human Barbie doll. In fact, *Playboy* blurred the distinction between the various sleek and sophisticated items of affluence that the magazine celebrated—cars, fashion, food, and drink—and the women it displayed.

Feminist Criticism

This objectification of women would raise the ire of feminists and the women's movement in the 1960s and 1970s. Targeting *Playboy* for its role in the degradation of women, feminists attacked the magazine for displaying "their girls as if they were a commodity," as Germaine Greer observed. Gloria Steinem, who had gone undercover for an exposé as Bunny Marie in the early 1960s, called the *Playboy* philosophy "boyish, undeveloped, anti-sensual, vicarious and sad." Susan Brownmiller, in her important study, *Against Our Will: Men, Women and Rape,* described the culture of pornography and rape that *Playboy,* in her view, helped to shape, by analyzing why women's response is so different from men's to the pictorials: It comes "from the gut knowledge that we and our bodies are being stripped, exposed, and contorted for the purpose of ridicule to bolster that 'masculine esteem' which gets its kick and sense of power from viewing females as anonymous, panting playthings, adult toys, dehumanized objects to be used, abused, broken, and discarded." In *Playboy*'s defense, Hefner has explained, "We've played a decontaminating role in changing attitudes toward nudity. The feminists who criticize us don't realize how *Playboy,* far more than the women's magazines, is responsible for the nongirdle look, the bikini, the miniskirt, the openness to nudity. . . . We've helped their movement in several ways."

In a sense, Hefner is both right and wrong. *Playboy* has certainly played a significant role in documenting and celebrating a new sexual freedom against past hypocritical and repressive customs and conventions. Yet the image of women that *Playboy* has made part of mainstream culture—prompting a host of imitators, like *Penthouse* and *Hustler,* that push even further to distort the distinction between the erotic and the pornographic—is an ambivalent legacy that enforces notions of women's submissiveness, the primacy of physicality, and gender inequality. To a question on *The Dick Cavett Show* in the early 1970s about her definition of sexual equality, Susan Brownmiller responded: "When Hugh Hefner comes out here with a cottontail attached to his rear end, then we'll have equality."

Playboy's Legacy

Playboy has over the years altered somewhat with the times, supporting the Equal Rights Amendment, abortion rights, and rape counseling. It has also been hurt by women's criticism, bad management decisions to expand beyond magazine publishing, and changing times. In the 1970s circulation fell to 2.5 million, and as Hefner later admitted, "We went through a period when we lost our bearings and started imitating the imitators." More suggestive poses, and implications of lesbianism and masturbation, caused conservative advertisers to withdraw their accounts. A management shake-up trimmed jobs and returned the focus of Playboy Enterprises to the magazine with less lurid sexual pictorials and a renewed emphasis on high-quality written content. The enterprise is now under the direct supervision of Hefner's daughter, Christie Hefner, who has stated that *Playboy* "has to deal with more ways of intercourse between the sexes than sexual." It is unclear, however, whether *Playboy* will be able to maintain its place in America's sexual psyche or whether its philosophy is now little more than a quaint reminder of an earlier, far less enlightened sexist time. Nevertheless, the appearance in 1953 of *Playboy* marked a major shift in raising the topic of sexuality to the center of the debate over cultural and social values and women's place in men's imagination.

CHAPTER 3

LIVING THROUGH
THE COLD WAR

Fighting for Rights

The Women's Movement Can Transform Society

Gloria Steinem

The women's liberation movement, which formed in 1969 as women worked within the civil rights movement, consisted of a loose network of women's groups opposed to a patriarchal (male-dominated) society. They challenged the notion that men should control all the public spheres while women should remain in the domestic sphere to keep house and raise children. Members of the movement led vigorous campaigns against pornography, rape, sexist language, and unequal pay. Betty Friedan's book The Feminine Mystique *and her founding of the National Organization for Women (NOW) in 1966 helped pave the way for the women's movement. One of the movement's mottos was "the personal is political," which meant that members felt their personal relationships with men reflected how power was unequally organized in society. The women's movement gained most of its momentum in the 1970s.*

Gloria Steinem is a leading spokesperson for women's rights. She was the founding editor of the feminist magazine Ms., *and her books include* Outrageous Acts and Everyday Rebellions *and a biography of Marilyn Monroe. In the following essay, written in 1970, Steinem predicts what America might be like if the women's movement triumphs. While she calls her predictions utopian, she is careful to stress her belief that the women's rights movement will not challenge established institutions like the family. Women do not want to replace men as the people in power, she insists; they simply want an egalitarian society.*

Any change is fearful, especially one affecting both politics and sex roles, so let me begin these utopian speculations with a fact. To break the ice.

Women don't want to exchange places with men. Male chauvinists, science-fiction writers and comedians may favor that idea for its shock value, but psychologists say it is a fantasy based on ruling-class ego and guilt. Men assume that women want to imitate them, which is just what white people assumed about blacks. An assumption so strong that it may convince the second-class group of the need to imitate, but for both women and blacks that stage has passed. Guilt produces the question: What if they could treat us as we have treated them?

That is not our goal. But we do want to change the economic system to one more based on merit. In Women's Lib Utopia, there will be free access to good jobs—and decent pay for the bad ones women have been performing all along, including housework. Increased skilled labor might lead to a four-hour workday, and higher wages would encourage further mechanization of repetitive jobs now kept alive by cheap labor.

With women as half the country's elected representatives, and a woman President once in a while, the country's *machismo* problems would be greatly reduced. The old-fashioned idea that manhood depends on violence and victory is, after all, an important part of our troubles in the streets, and in Viet Nam. I'm not saying that women leaders would eliminate violence. We are not more moral than men; we are only uncorrupted by power so far. When we do acquire power, we might turn out to have an equal impulse toward aggression. Even now, Margaret Mead [American anthropologist noted for her studies of sexual behavior in primitive cultures] believes that women fight less often but more fiercely than men, because women are not taught the rules of the war game and fight only when cornered. But for the next 50 years or so, women in politics will be very valuable by tempering the idea of manhood into something less aggressive and better suited to this crowded, post-atomic planet. Consumer protection and children's rights, for instance, might get more legislative attention.

Men will have to give up ruling-class privileges, but in return they will no longer be the only ones to support the family, get drafted, bear the strain of power and responsibility. [Sigmund] Freud [who focused on the importance of the phallus] to the contrary, anatomy is not destiny, at least not for more than nine months at a time. In Israel, women are drafted, and some have gone to war. In England, more men type and run switchboards. In India and Israel, a woman rules. In Sweden, both parents take care of the children. In this country, come Utopia, men and women won't reverse roles; they will be free to choose according to individual talents and preferences.

If role reform sounds sexually unsettling, think how it will change the sexual hypocrisy we have now. No more sex arranged on the barter system, with women pretending interest, and men never sure whether they are loved for themselves or for the security few women can get any other way. (Married or not, for sexual reasons or social ones, most women still find it second nature to Uncle-Tom.[1]) No more men who are encouraged to spend a lifetime living with inferiors; with housekeepers, or dependent creatures who are still children. No more domineering wives, emasculating women, and "Jewish mothers," all of whom are simply human beings with all their normal ambition and drive confined to the home. No more unequal partnerships that eventually doom love and sex.

In order to produce that kind of confidence and individuality, child rearing will train according to talent. Little girls will no longer be surrounded by air-tight, self-fulfilling prophecies of natural passivity, lack of ambition and objectivity,

1. a reference to a black character in the novel *Uncle Tom's Cabin*, who is excessively subservient to whites

inability to exercise power, and dexterity (so long as special aptitude for jobs requiring patience and dexterity is confined to poorly paid jobs; brain surgery is for males).

Schools and universities will help to break down traditional sex roles, even when parents will not. Half the teachers will be men, a rarity now at preschool and elementary levels; girls will not necessarily serve cookies or boys hoist up the flag. Athletic teams will be picked only by strength and skill. Sexually segregated courses like auto mechanics and home economics will be taken by boys and girls together. New courses in sexual politics will explore female subjugation as the model for political oppression, and women's history will be an academic staple, along with black history, at least until the white-male-oriented textbooks are integrated and rewritten.

As for the American child's classic problem—too much mother, too little father—that would be cured by an equalization of parental responsibility. Free nurseries, school lunches, family cafeterias built into every housing complex, service companies that will do household cleaning chores in a regular, businesslike way, and more responsibility by the entire community for the children: all these will make it possible for both mother and father to work, and to have equal leisure time with the children at home. For parents of very young children, however, a special job category, created by Government and unions, would allow such parents a shorter work day.

The revolution would not take away the option of being a housewife. A woman who prefers to be her husband's housekeeper and/or hostess would receive a percentage of his pay determined by the domestic relations courts. If divorced, she might be eligible for a pension fund, and for a job-training allowance. Or a divorce could be treated the same way that the dissolution of a business partnership is now.

If these proposals seem farfetched, consider Sweden, where most of them are already in effect. Sweden is not yet a working Women's Lib model; most of the role-reform programs began less than a decade ago, and are just beginning to take hold. But that country is so far ahead of us in recognizing the problem that Swedish statements on sex and equality sound like bulletins from the moon.

Our marriage laws, for instance, are so reactionary that Women's Lib groups want couples to take a compulsory written exam on the law, as for a driver's license, before going through with the wedding. A man has alimony and wifely debts to worry about, but a woman may lose so many of her civil rights that in the U.S. now, in important legal ways, she becomes a child again. In some states, she cannot sign credit agreements, use her maiden name, incorporate a business, or establish a legal residence of her own. Being a wife, according to most social and legal definitions, is still a 19th century thing.

Assuming, however, that these blatantly sexist laws are abolished or reformed, that job discrimination is forbidden, that parents share financial responsibility for each other and the children, and that sexual relationships become partnerships of equal adults (some pretty big assumptions), then marriage will probably go right on. Men and women are, after all, physically complementary. When society stops encouraging men to be exploiters and women to be parasites, they may turn out to be more complementary in emotion as well. Women's Lib is not trying to destroy the American family. A look at the statistics on divorce—plus the way in which old people are farmed out with strangers and young people flee the home—shows the destruction that has already been done. Liberated women are just trying to point out the disaster, and build compassionate and practical alternatives from the ruins.

What will exist is a variety of alternative life-styles. Since the population explosion dictates that childbearing be kept to a minimum, parents-and-children will be only one of many "families": couples, age groups, working groups, mixed communes, blood-related clans, class groups, creative groups. Single women will have the right to stay single without ridicule, without the attitudes now betrayed by "spinster" and "bachelor." Lesbians or homosexuals will no longer be denied legally binding marriages, complete with mutual-support agreements and inheritance rights. Paradoxically, the number of homosexuals may get smaller. With fewer overpossessive mothers and fewer fathers who hold up an impossibly cruel or perfectionist idea of manhood, boys will be less likely to be denied or reject their identity as males.

Changes that now seem small may get bigger:

Men's lib. Men now suffer from more diseases due to stress, heart attacks, ulcers, a higher suicide rate, greater difficulty living alone, less adaptability to change and, in general, a shorter life span than women. There is some scientific evidence that what produces physical problems is not work itself, but the inability to choose which work, and how much. With women bearing half the financial responsibility, and with the idea of "masculine" jobs gone, men might well feel freer and live longer.

Religion. Protestant women are already becoming ordained ministers; radical nuns are carrying out liturgical functions that were once the exclusive property of priests: Jewish women are rewriting prayers—particularly those that Orthodox Jews recite every morning thanking God they are not female. In the future, the church will become an area of equal participation by women. This means, of course, that organized religion will have to give up one of its great historical weapons: sexual repression. In most structured faiths, from Hinduism through Roman Catholicism, the status of women went down as the position of priests ascended. Male clergy implied, if they did not teach, that women were unclean, unworthy and sources of ungodly temptation, in order to remove them as rivals for the emotional forces of men. Full participation of women in ecclesiastical life might involve certain changes in theology, such as, for instance, a radical redefinition of sin.

Literary problems. Revised sex roles will outdate more children's books than civil rights ever did. Only a few children had the problem of a *Little Black Sambo,* but most have the male-female stereotypes of "Dick and Jane." A boomlet of children's books about mothers who work has already begun, and liberated parents and editors are beginning to pressure for change in the textbook industry. Fiction writing will change more gradually, but romantic novels with wilting heroines and swashbuckling heroes will be reduced to historical value. Or perhaps to the sado-masochist trade. (*Marjorie Morningstar,* a romantic novel that took the '50s by storm, has already begun to seem as unreal as its '20s predecessor, *The Sheik.*) As for the literary plots that turn on forced marriages or horrific abortions, they will seem as dated as Prohibition stories. Free legal abortions and free birth control will force writers to give up pregnancy as the *deus ex machina* [a sudden and unexpected solution to a problem].

Manners and fashion. Dress will be more androgynous, with class symbols becoming more important than sexual ones. Pro- or anti-Establishment styles may already be more vital than who is wearing them. Hardhats are just as likely to rough up antiwar girls as antiwar men in the street, and police understand that women are just as likely to be pushers or bombers. Dances haven't required that one partner lead the other for years, anyway. Chivalry [often exemplified by opening a door for another person] will transfer itself to those who need it, or deserve respect: old people, admired people, anyone with an armload of packages. Women with normal work identities will be less likely to attach their whole sense of self to youth and appearance; thus there will be fewer nervous breakdowns when the first wrinkles appear. Lighting [someone else's] cigarettes and other treasured niceties will become gestures of mutual affection. "I like to be helped on with my coat," says one Women's Lib worker, "but not if it costs me $2,000 a year in salary."

For those with nostalgia for a simpler past, here is a word of comfort. Anthropologist Geoffrey Gorer studied the few peaceful human tribes and discovered one common characteristic: sex roles were not polarized. Differences of dress and occupation were at a minimum. Society, in other words, was not using sexual blackmail as a way of getting women to do cheap labor, or men to be aggressive.

Thus Women's Lib may achieve a more peaceful society on the way toward its other goals. That is why the Swedish government considers reform to bring about greater equality in the sex roles one of its most important concerns. As Prime Minister Olof Palme explained in a widely ignored speech delivered in Washington this spring [1970]: "It is *human beings* we shall emancipate. In Sweden today, if a politician should declare that the woman ought to have a different role from man's, he would be regarded as something from the Stone Age." In other words, the most radical goal of the movement is egalitarianism.

If Women's Lib wins, perhaps we all do.

The Stonewall Riots and the Birth of the Gay Rights Movement

Richard Goldstein

Police raids on gay bars were fairly common across America until the late 1960s. Patrons at these establishments were arrested on indecency charges for holding hands, kissing, cross-dressing, or simply being present. Often their identities were published in newspapers. On June 28, 1969, one such raid occurred at a New York City gay bar called the Stonewall Inn, sparking weeks of violent conflicts between homosexuals and police. The riots marked the first time a significant number of homosexuals resisted such harassment.

In the following article Richard Goldstein describes the night of June 28 and the following days. He contends that the riots were a major catalyst for the gay rights movement and other social movements of the ensuing decades. Goldstein is the former editor of the Village Voice *and the author of the book* The Attack Queers: Liberal Society and Gay Rights.

A friend from Washington, D.C., wanted to see the landmarks of gay liberation in Greenwich Village. So I walked him down Christopher Street, past the Oscar Wilde Memorial Bookshop, with its window display of movement regalia and in-your-face T-shirts. I showed him the *Gay Liberation* sculpture by George Segal that had been installed on Sheridan Square, after a fierce fight with local conservatives. I pointed out the street sign the city had put up, dubbing the block we were strolling down STONEWALL PLACE. Across the street was a joint called the Stonewall, blazoning its name in red neon. How tacky, my friend remarked, for a gay bar here to call itself that.

I was reminded of how revered the word "Stonewall" has become. Gay people name everything from political clubs to brokerage firms after this site of the riots that sparked the modern gay movement. Yet little is known about the Stonewall Inn and the rebellion that occurred there in 1969. Indeed, my friend from Washington had no idea that the bar whose name offended him is doing business in the same space as the original Stonewall.

In the intervening years, the joint went through several retail incarnations before regaining something of its former identity. The current owners have spiffed up the interior and strung a pair of rainbow flags from the façade, attracting a far more prosperous clientele than the crowd that spent time at the Stonewall in its heyday. But the brick façade is the same, and so is the large plate-glass window facing the sidewalk, though in 1969 it was backed with plywood and painted black.

The Stonewall Inn, 1969

Back then, the Stonewall Inn was the sort of semi-private "bottle bar" where flamers [flamboyant gays] were welcome, although the bouncer put a premium on gender-appropriate attire and a youthful mien. The drinks were watered down, and there was no sink at the bar; used glasses were dunked in a barrel of bilge and refilled for the next customer. But in an era when same-sex dancing was a criminal act, the black-lit floor with its tinny music system and go-go dancer in a gilded cage was the closest thing to a gay disco.

Elsewhere in the Village, there were bars for drag queens and leather men, but no type ruled the Stonewall. College kids mingled with lowlife: all races and classes unwound in this disco demimonde, The police—known by the clientele as Betty Badge or Lily Law—visited occasionally, but they usually arrived before the big crowds, and left promptly without making arrests. After all, the Stonewall was a cash cow for the mafiosi who ran it and the cops they paid off.

The Bust

But early Saturday morning, June 28, 1969, detectives descended on the bar at the peak hour of 1 A.M., without informing the management in advance. White lights came up on the dance floor, signaling the male couples to separate. After enduring insults and humiliating ID checks, most of the customers were shown the door. Only the drag queens were detained, as was customary in those days. As they were led to a waiting paddy wagon, they struck fabulous poses for the crowd that had gathered on the street. It was a time-honored ritual in Greenwich Village, but on this night something was different. The police were oblivious to the electricity and unaware of the intense emotions generated by Judy Garland's [American singer-actress best known for her role as Dorothy in *The Wizard of Oz*] funeral, which had drawn thousands of gay mourners earlier that day.

Some say a lesbian threw the first punch at Lily Law; others claim the drag queens fought back. Soon the crowd was pelting the police with coins, as if to say, Take your cut and get out. "By now, the crowd had swelled to a mob," writes historian Martin Duberman in his . . . book, *Stonewall,* the first detailed account of the riot that ensued. "People were picking up and throwing whatever loose objects came to hand—coins, bottles, cans, bricks . . . even . . . dog s— from the street." The police retreated into the bar, where they were trapped. Cornered with them was a *Village Voice* reporter, who found the experience "very scary. Very enlightening."

Angry Rioters

As the crowd surged against the door, someone poured lighter fluid through the broken window and ignited a blaze. The cops turned on a fire hose and tried to clear a path to the street, but escaped only when a backup force arrived. "I had been in combat situations," said the deputy inspector in charge of the raid, "[but] there was never any time that I felt more scared."

What shocked this seasoned officer was the pent-up rage of people no longer willing to accept the usual abuse. No one thought these pansies were capable of resistance, not even homosexual activists from the Mattachine Society [an organization founded in 1955 to educate the public on homosexuality] who watched from a distance, stunned. Later, they would plead with the gay community to uphold law and order, even as more militant activists toured the bars shouting, "Out of the closets and into the streets."

As the night unfolded, the crowd swelled to thousands, until, finally, the Tactical Patrol Force arrived. This riot squad had been honed on anti-war protests, and its members were helmeted and heavily armed. As they marched up Christopher Street in a Roman wedge formation, the crowd retreated, but bolted up the side streets and regrouped behind the police, pelting them with debris. As Duberman writes, the cops "found themselves face to face with their worst nightmare," a chorus line of queens, kicking their heels in the air and singing: "We are the Stonewall girls/ We wear our hair in curls/ We wear no underwear/ We show our pubic hair. . . ."

The riots continued well into the following week, attracting the queer and the curious from all over town. Fingers were severed and faces smashed by the cops, who were in turn kicked, bitten, and coated with the contents of a garbage can. Night after night, a new cry echoed through the streets of the Village: "Gay power." By the time things calmed down, much more than the etiquette of policing gay bars had changed. Almost instantaneously, a new cadre was formed, calling itself the Gay Liberation Front and allying itself with the Black Panthers and other struggles of the time.

Gay Power and Change

Plans were laid for the city's first gay pride march (held, to this day, on the anniversary of the Stonewall riots). [New

York] Mayor [John] Lindsay and the American Psychiatric Association were among the targets of spontaneous protests—known as "zaps"— and even the *Village Voice* received a visit from what one of its writers had called "the forces of faggotry." As the movement expanded, thousands of homosexuals who had made their peace with society through isolation and a painful discretion realized they were part of a dynamic and overt community. Extensive coverage by the New York dailies spread the word, and the energies unleashed by Stonewall rippled out across the country. Soon there were dozens of gay organizations, then hundreds, then thousands.

The spirit of Stonewall has infused much more than the gay-liberation movement. Its echo can be heard in the refusal of AIDS activists to go gently into that plague night; in the rejection by disabled Americans of the limits created by stigma; and in the feminist demand for self-definition and freedom from male authority. The Stonewall rebellion changed the face of activist politics. It taught us to value the vision of society's most degraded members, to be wary of leaders, and to put our faith in the power of spontaneous action. Most important, Stonewall affirmed a timeless American lesson: Identity is not something you are born into; it's something you discover, through love and action.

The Difficulty of Coming Out as a Lesbian During the Revolution

Boston Gay Collective

Though the 1960s and the sexual revolution were times of great change, there was still much popular resistance to homosexuality. Gay and lesbian Americans saw little change in their reception by society even by the end of the decade. The Women's Movement was a great source of help to lesbians as they struggled to identify with their sexuality.

The Boston Gay Collective provides the following first-person accounts of what it was like to come out and become openly lesbian at the end of the sixties. These narratives appeared in the book Our Bodies, Ourselves *(1971) that was assembled by the Boston Women's Health Book Collective, a nonprofit, public interest women's health education, advocacy, and consulting organization. The book has been both praised by those who support gay rights and attacked by religious conservatives who believe homosexuality is immoral.*

Sarah. I'm twenty-eight, and I "came out" when I slept with a friend four years ago [1972]. But it took me about six months to actively assert my gay identity. I understood my reluctance to being labeled "lesbian" after listening to a couple of gay women at a gay bar react violently to the word. They saw themselves as human beings, not as labels. But, I thought, that's just not the way people deal with each other in this society. They give you labels whether you take them or not. They reminded me too much of myself ten or fifteen years ago, when I responded similarly to being called a Jew.

The Boston Women's Health Book Collective, *Our Bodies, Ourselves, 2nd Edition, Revised.* New York: Simon and Schuster, 1976. Copyright © 1976 by The Boston Women's Health Book Collective, Inc. Reproduced by permission of Simon & Schuster Adult Publishing Group; in the United Kingdom by Penguin Books, Ltd.

From the sixth grade on, I was the only Jew in my school. Everyone informed me of that, and it was no compliment coming from their mouths. I thought of myself as smart, capable, good at science and math. I was going to be another Marie Curie. But I was also intimidated by other peoples' judgments; I had to figure out how to fit in. "No, we don't bury our dead standing up," I would say. I really wanted to have friends, and I did get close to girls and boys. But I was always on the fence; they might always turn around and say "You're a Jew." This explains a lot of my reluctance to identify myself as gay and say "I'm a lesbian."

Resisting Labels

I thought I could have what people would call a gay relationship with my friend and not have to get into gay women's liberation or see myself as a lesbian. I had the choice not to do that. I knew by calling myself a lesbian I was asking for disapproval, distance and perhaps violence from most people. And since I had gone through it once, why ask for it again? So for a long time I did not identify. Then I realized that while ideally no one wants to be labeled, I do live in a society where people react to each other that way, and I don't have any control over that. I can't deny how people relate to me. Yes, I'm Jewish and I'm a lesbian.

I'm one of those women who "came out" with the women's movement. Women's Liberation made me think about my past, about when I was a kid and liked to play football and baseball. To me the accusation "You throw like a girl" was a terrible put-down—I didn't want to be lumped in the "girl" category. I realized when thinking about my family that my parents had similar expectations for me and my brother— except that I was urged to be nice, considerate, concerned for others in ways my brother was rarely pressed to show.

Youth and Gender

I thought about how, in junior high, the boys looked at the

girls as developing bodies. They would yell, "Pearl Harbor, surprise attack!" as they grabbed our breasts and forced us down on the ground to get the "big feel." I know it scared me then, but how could I deal with my anger and fear when what was so important among girls was to be accepted by the boys? And having a boyfriend was often a protection from those other boys.

In ninth grade a group of girls got close. We used to hug and kiss each other a lot and have slumber parties. Most of us had boyfriends, but we were very important to each other. Once in a while someone would say, "What are you, a homo?" and we'd laugh. It didn't mean anything and it didn't change our behavior in any way.

Examining Sexuality

That's the only reference to homosexuality that I can remember before college. In college I got hit with [Sigmund] Freud [recognized as the founder of psychoanalysis] and latent homosexual tendencies. What did this mean for me, who had always been more emotionally attached to women than to men? In freshman year my roommate and I became very close and dependent on each other, but neither of us could handle the intensity; that happened to me a lot with female friends. In psychotherapy I asked (indirectly of course) if I had "those tendencies." After about fifteen minutes the therapist figured out the question and asked, "Are you wondering if you're a lesbian?" Me: "Not really—ahh, I'm just wondering what you think about those tendencies." "You've given no indications of that," he said. Phew! was my reaction, not knowing what those "indications" were. (That's a story of how expertise has power over people's lives.) So I didn't worry about being a lesbian, but continued to build close friendships with women.

Valuing Female Relationships

After college I felt the sadness of women friends going in different directions without the question of sharing our lives, as there would be with boyfriends. I went with a guy for three years, but he was never more important to me than two of my female friends. That was to my liking, not his. He wanted to get married, but since marriage wasn't part of any world I could imagine for myself we split up. Sometimes my friendships with women were threatened by their jealous boyfriends. With these feelings, I could no longer ignore the women's movement. I read something another woman had written about her—and my—experiences. Fantastic! I wasn't alone. I began thinking that men didn't understand friendship, that they were sexual prowlers wanting all the attention focused on them; whereas my relationships with women seemed natural, exciting and intense.

Working with Women's Liberation in Boston meant being with women all the time. A group of us who weren't really close but were friends would hang out together, circle-dance at a bar, play basketball. Diana was one of them. She and I found we could tune into each other's survival tactics. What a relief. We could accept each other without many hurt feelings; we shared a lot of interests and criticisms of the women's movement. Eventually we slept together. That was four years ago.

Growing Up with Anxiety

Diana. When I was a kid, I was always a tomboy. In seventh grade the situation changed—I went to a private school where I didn't know anyone and all my friends were girls. I never got to know any of the boys and couldn't see why anyone would want to—they were picking on younger kids, harassing women teachers, and so on. It seemed as though you couldn't get to know them as friends, but only flirt with them. I didn't want to flirt, so I didn't go to parties everyone else was going to. I knew of course that when boys and girls grew up they were supposed to mysteriously start being attracted to each other. I thought that would happen to me too, later. But the kids in my class just seemed to be playing at being grown up.

In junior high I started identifying more strongly as a girl. Boys were becoming more and more of an alien group. I still hated stockings and frills, but I certainly didn't want to be a boy any more.

We had dancing classes in junior high. One night between dances a cold breeze started blowing through the open window. I reached over and touched Margaret's knee and asked her if she was getting cold, too. She shrank back in mock horror and said, "What's the matter, Diana, are you a lesbian?" Everyone nearby started snickering. I didn't know what a lesbian was, but I knew I didn't want to be one. Later I found out; there was a lot of joking and taunting among girls in my class about lesbianism, which they viewed as sick and disgusting.

Resisting Feelings

I went to an all-girls boarding school for high school. I was happy to be in an all-girls school because I thought of boys as people you couldn't act naturally with, people who would make the classroom atmosphere tense and uptight. I began to worry consciously about being a lesbian. I knew that wherever I went, women attracted my attention, never men. If I rode on a bus or subway I would watch the faces of all the women. My emotional attachments were all to women, and I had crushes on women friends. But I thought that if my attachments weren't sexual I was okay. I tried imagining sex with one of the seniors and was repelled by the thought. That was a relief. I said to myself that I was attracted to girls' *faces*, not their bodies. I told myself, "I just think Kitty's body is beautiful from an *esthetic* point of view, not a sexual one."

I was a tactophobe—a word we invented to mean someone who was afraid of touching people. I was afraid that if I touched other girls I would like it and keep on touching them. So I became repulsed at the idea, to save myself from perversion.

I went to college, and as I began sleeping with boys, I began to lose some of my fear of being a lesbian. I enjoyed sex with boys at first, though I didn't much enjoy being with them otherwise and was always trying to think up reasons not to see my boyfriend. I thought men were boring, and I still felt I had to act very artificially with them.

I began to go on a campaign to become more boy-oriented. I tried consciously to watch more men and fewer women in the subway. I wanted to feel turned on to men, not because it would be enjoyable, but because I was afraid I would not be a complete woman otherwise.

A Different Culture

One summer I went to Latin America. There the women are much more physical with each other, walking arm in arm, dancing close together, and touching each other more. I liked this freedom and thought that it showed how culture-bound our definitions of homosexuality are. I got close to one woman, a nurse named Edna. Before I left I spent a day at her house. We were sitting on her bed and she started sucking my finger. I was totally turned on. As I left I thought, Oh, no, there's no denying it any more. I'm a lesbian. Bisexuality did not occur to me as a possibility, although I knew the term. I thought if I was turned on to women, I must accept the fact of being a total queer.

I got into the women's movement and felt an enormous relief that I would no longer have to play roles with men and act feminine and sweet, dress in skirts and heels, and do all the things I'd done on dates. Then I began to feel hatred for men for having forced me into these roles. During this time, I would buy women's papers as soon as they came out and look immediately for articles by gay women. I began to hang out with gay women, who turned out to be regular people, not the stereotypes I had imagined. On a gut level I was beginning to realize that gayness was not a sickness. One night I went out for a long walk, and when I got home I had decided I was a lesbian. For me it was not a decision to become a lesbian. It was a question of accepting and becoming comfortable with feelings that I had always had.

The Importance of the Women's Movement

I don't know if I would ever have come out if it hadn't been for the women's movement. The women's movement first led me to question the "naturalness" of the male-female roles that I had always largely accepted. Because I thought that role-playing heterosexuality was "the way it's supposed to be," whenever I rebelled against these roles I was afraid that this meant I was not a complete woman, that there was something wrong with me—not enough sex hormones, no doubt. The women's movement helped me to reject these roles, and with them every reason for struggling to be heterosexual. I realized femaleness was something I was born with; it was not something others could reward me with when I acted "feminine," or take away from me as a punishment.

Overturning Laws Against Mixed-Race Marriages

Robert A. Pratt

In 1967 laws against interracial marriage still existed in sixteen states. Richard and Mildred Loving lived in one of these states, Virginia. In 1958 they traveled to Washington, D.C., to be married. However, they were arrested shortly after their return to Virginia, where their marriage was void. The couple challenged the conviction all the way to the U.S. Supreme Court, which overturned the antimiscegenation law, thereby setting a precedent for other states to do so as well.

Richard A. Pratt, who lived next to the Lovings as a child, relates in this personal narrative the details leading up to the Supreme Court ruling. He highlights the prejudice the Lovings met with and also the complex racial relations of the South in the late 1960s. Pratt heads the history department at the University of Georgia and is the author of The Color of Their Skin: Education and Race in Richmond, Virginia, 1954–1989 *(1992) and* We Shall Not Be Moved: The Desegregation of the University of Georgia *(2002).*

On many evenings just before sunset, my grandmother and I would sit on our front porch. We lived in the rural black community of Battery, Virginia (approximately forty-five miles east of Richmond), which is located in Essex County. Suddenly, I would hear my grandmother remark: "Well, I see Richard's gone in for the night." I would then turn my head to follow the direction of her gaze, where I would see a white man driving his car down the dirt road leading to a house owned by my great-uncle. It was a two-story wood-frame house, which was one of the biggest in the neighborhood.

Most of the rooms were usually rented out to various family friends, relatives, and occasionally to the families of those who worked at the sawmill—jointly operated by my great-uncle and his older brother, my grandfather.

Raymond and Garnet Hill, along with their two sons, lived there for a time in the early 1960s. Garnet's younger sister, Mildred, was a frequent visitor, especially on weekends. Mildred's three children usually accompanied her on these visits, but her husband never did—at least not during daylight hours. As my grandmother later explained, the white man who occasionally visited my great-uncle's house near nightfall was Richard Loving. The woman whom I knew as Mildred was his wife, and the three children with whom I occasionally played were their children.

Restraints on Relationships

If Richard Loving was to spend any time with his family in the state of Virginia, he had no choice other than to do so under the cover of darkness. He and his part-black, part-Cherokee wife had been banned from the state in 1959 for violating the state's miscegenation laws, which prohibited interracial marriage. Although Richard Loving and Mildred Jeter were legally married in Washington, D.C., in 1958, Virginia did not recognize the marriage and subsequently banned the couple from their native state. Not until 1967, when the United States Supreme Court declared Virginia's miscegenation statutes unconstitutional in *Loving v. Virginia,* were Richard and Mildred Loving allowed to return to the state of their birth, having spent the first five years of their marriage in exile.

Richard Perry Loving and Mildred Delores Jeter had known each other practically all of their lives, as their families lived just up the road from each other in the rural community of Central Point, Virginia, located in Caroline County. Central Point had developed an interesting history of black-white sexual relationships over the years, which over time had produced a community in which a considerable number of the blacks were light-skinned. Some of the blacks in the area who were light enough to "pass" as white often did so, and some of those whose complexion was a little darker often claimed to be Native American, even though most of them were known to have black relatives. While there is undoubtedly a Native American presence in Caroline County, not everyone who claimed to be an "Indian" really was, but given the racial climate of the 1950s, some blacks thought it more socially acceptable to emphasize their Native American rather than their African ancestry.

An Accepting Community

Richard Loving spent most of his time in the company of these light-skinned blacks, who accepted him warmly, in part because his whiteness validated theirs but also because Richard's parents had lived among these people for most of their lives without asserting any of the prerogatives generally associated with white supremacy. For twenty-three years, Richard's father had defied the racial mores of southern white society by working for Boyd Byrd, one of the wealthiest black farmers in the community; and apparently, he never had any qualms about doing so. While the elder Lovings were not oblivious to racial differences, the close-knit nature of their community required a certain degree of interdependence which could sometimes lead to an acceptance of personal relationships in a particular setting that would have been anathema elsewhere. So when white Richard Loving, age seventeen, began courting "colored" Mildred Jeter, age eleven, their budding romance drew little attention from either the white or the black community.

Mildred (part black and part Cherokee) had a pretty light-brown complexion accentuated by her slim figure, which was why practically everyone who knew her called her "Stringbean," or "Bean" for short. Richard (part English and part Irish) was a brick-layer by trade but spent much of his spare time drag-racing a car that he co-owned with two black friends, Raymond Green (a mechanic) and Percy Fortune (a local merchant). Despite their natural shyness, both Richard and Mildred were well liked in the community, and the fact that they attended different churches and different schools did not hinder their courtship. When he was twenty-four and she was eighteen, Richard and Mildred decided to legalize their relationship by getting married.

Violating the Law and Leaving Virginia

Mildred did not know that interracial marriage was illegal in Virginia, but Richard did. This explains why, on June 2, 1958, he drove them across the Virginia state line to Washington, D.C., to be married. With their union legally validated by the District of Columbia, Mr. and Mrs. Loving returned to Central Point to live with Mildred's parents; however, their marital bliss was short-lived. Five weeks later, on July 11, their quiet life was shattered when they were awakened early in the morning as three law officers "acting on an anonymous tip" opened the unlocked door of their home, walked into their bedroom, and shined a flashlight in their faces. Caroline County Sheriff R. Garnett Brooks demanded to know what the two of them were doing in bed together. Mildred answered, "I'm his wife," while Richard pointed to the District of Columbia marriage certificate that hung on their bedroom wall. "That's no good here," Sheriff Brooks replied. He charged the couple with unlawful cohabitation, and then he and his two deputies hauled the Lovings off to a nearby jail in Bowling Green.

At its October term in 1958, a grand jury issued indictments against the couple for violating Virginia's ban on interracial marriages. Specifically, they were charged with violating Virginia's 1924 Racial Integrity Act. The act stipulated that all marriages between a white person and a colored person shall be absolutely void without any decree of divorce or other legal process, and it prohibited interracial couples from circumventing the law by having their marriages validated elsewhere and later return[ing] to Virginia. The Lovings waived their rights to a trial by jury and pled guilty to the charges. On January 6, 1959, Judge Leon M. Bazile sentenced each of them to one year in jail, but he suspended the sentences on the condition that they leave the state of Virginia and not return together or at the same time for a period of twenty-five years. The Lovings paid their court fees of $36.29 each and moved to Washington, D.C., where they would spend their next five years in exile.

Living in Exile

During their years in the nation's capital, the Lovings lived with Mildred's cousin Alex Byrd and his wife, Laura, at 1151 Neal Street, Northeast. Their first child, Sidney, was born in 1958; Donald was born in 1959; and Peggy, the only girl, was born in 1960. The years in Washington were not happy ones for the couple. Richard struggled to maintain permanent employment while Mildred busied herself tending to the needs of their three children. During this time, they remained oblivious to the civil rights movement that was unfolding in their midst. "I just missed being at home," she told me years later. "I missed being with my family and friends, especially Garnet [her sister]. I wanted my children to grow up in the country, where they could run and play, and where I wouldn't worry about them so much. I never liked much about the city."

Virginia law would not allow Richard and Mildred Loving to live together as husband and wife in the state, nor would they be allowed to raise their mixed race children (considered illegitimate under state law) in Virginia. They could visit Virginia, but they could not do so together. They were not even allowed to be in the state at the same time; however, that did not stop them from trying or from succeeding on various occasions. Mildred and the children made frequent visits to Battery, Virginia, the rural black community where her sister and brother-in-law lived. When Mildred would arrive in Battery, some of the neighbors would begin to look at their watches to see how long it would be before Richard's car came cruising through the neighborhood. During those early years, Richard's visits to the "Big House" (the common nickname for my great-uncle's boarding house) occurred almost exclusively after dark; but after a time he became less cautious. Perhaps he was confident in the belief that our community would keep his secret, or he was convinced that the local authorities in Essex County (which was adjacent to Caroline County) were not that interested in monitoring his whereabouts. It was on those occasions that I played with the Loving children, especially Sidney, who was exactly my age.

Challenging the Ruling

The Lovings had not really been that interested in the civil rights movement, nor had they ever given much thought to challenging Virginia's law. But with a major civil rights bill being debated in Congress in 1963, Mildred decided to write to Robert Kennedy, the Attorney General of the United States. The Department of Justice referred the letter to the American Civil Liberties Union (ACLU). Bernard S. Cohen, a young lawyer doing pro bono work for the ACLU in Alexandria, Virginia, agreed to take the case. He would later be joined by another young attorney, Philip J. Hirschkop.

In October 1964, Cohen and Hirschkop filed a class action suit in the U.S. District Court for the Eastern District of Virginia. In January 1965, Judge Bazile presided over a hearing of the Lovings' petition to have his original decision set aside. In a written opinion, he rebutted each of the contentions made by Cohen and Hirschkop that might have resulted in a reconsideration of their clients' guilt. After citing several legal precedents he concluded: "Almighty God created the races white, black, yellow, malay and red, and he placed them on separate continents. And but for the interference with his arrangement, there would be no cause for such marriages. The fact that he separated the races shows that he did not intend for the races to mix." The Lovings' attorneys appealed to the Virginia Supreme Court of Appeals, but their luck was no better there. On March 7, 1966, a unanimous court upheld Judge Bazile's decision. The convictions remained intact. Having exhausted their appeals in Virginia's courts, the Lovings proceeded to the U.S. Supreme Court.

To the Supreme Court

On December 12, 1966, the U.S. Supreme Court agreed to hear the case. The [National Association for the Advancement of Colored People] (NAACP), the NAACP Legal Defense and Education Fund, the Japanese American Citizens League, and a coalition of Catholic bishops also submitted briefs on the couple's behalf. In preparing the brief for their clients, Cohen and Hirschkop reviewed the history of Virginia's miscegenation statutes dating back to the seventeenth century, referring to them as "relics of slavery" and "expressions of modern day racism." In concluding his oral argument on April 10, 1967, Cohen relayed a message to the justices from Richard Loving: "Tell the Court I love my wife, and it is just unfair that I can't live with her in Virginia."

CHAPTER 4

Evaluating the
Sexual Revolution

Criticizing the Sexual Revolution

Pitirim A. Sorokin

During the sexual revolution, books like Helen Gurley Brown's Sex and the Single Girl *and events like Jefferson Poland's nude "wade-in" gained a lot of attention. Nevertheless, it would be extremely inaccurate to say that the majority of America was being swayed toward the more liberal sexuality of a Brown or Poland. On the contrary, the conservative values of the fifties remained prominent.*

Pitirim A. Sorokin was a strong voice in opposition to the sexual revolution. Sorokin emigrated from Russia to America and eventually chaired the sociology department at Harvard. He wrote the books Social and Cultural Mobility *and* The Sociology of Revolution. *In the following excerpt from his 1956 book* The American Sex Revolution, *Sorokin compares America's growing sex addiction to drug addiction in the way that it causes people to lose sight of all moral and religious values outside. He says that the increased intensity of the sexual drive has had an effect on the overall culture of America: literature encourages lust while seductive jazz music consists mainly of sexual innuendo. Most importantly, Sorokin feels that the country is not paying attention to this decline in values, which is causing the family unit to deteriorate.*

Increasing divorce and desertion and the growth of prenuptial and extramarital sex relations are signs of sex addiction somewhat similar to drug addiction.

Through the use of drugs an addict strives to relieve his painful tensions and to experience the intensest forms of sensual pleasure. The more one indulges in the use of the drugs,

Pitirim A. Sorokin, *The American Sex Revolution*. Boston: Porter Sargent, 1956. Copyright © 1956 by F. Porter Sargent; renewed in 1984 by Sergei Sorokin and Peter Sorokin. Reproduced by permission of the Literary Estate of Pitirim A. Sorokin.

the deeper he is caught by their tentacles. The more he uses them, the more substantially they change the total personality of the drug addict.

Sex addiction does not represent an exception to these rules. Dedication of an individual to the pursuit of sex pleasures means a growth of the sex drive at the expense of the power of other factors determining his total activity, and radically changes the whole system of forces governing human behavior. It is similar to a change of an engine and of the total motor mechanism of a car. Externally the car may look the same, but its inner system and driving performance become quite different from what they were before. Likewise, a tangible modification of the system of forces conditioning human behavior transforms the total personality of the individual, his body and mind, his values and actions. The deeper this change, the greater the transformation of the person involved.

A Technical Explanation

This means that changes in the sex behavior of our men and women presuppose a parallel change of their biological and psychosocial properties, of their scientific, philosophical, religious, moral, aesthetic, and social values; and, also, a change of the comparative motivational effectiveness of each of these factor-values. The central biological transformation consists of a set of anatomical and physiological modifications that result in an over-excitation of sex appetite and sex activities. This over-stimulation may be due either to biological (glandular, and other) alterations in the organism, or to the changes in the psychological factors that inhibit and control sex impulses and activities. If, for instance, the motivational control and inhibition of these psychosocial factors weakens, or if instead of inhibiting, they begin to approve, glorify, and justify the greater and more promiscuous sex freedom, the biological sex drive becomes progressively disinhibited and acquires a much greater "motivational power" in propelling the individual toward less and less restrained sex relations. In almost all sex revolutions on a mass scale, the increase of motivational power of the sex drive is due mainly to the weakening of the controls of the psychosocial factors or values, and the replacement of the inhibitive psychosocial factor-values by those that approve sex passion, sex prowess, and more varied sex relations.

This seems to be true also of the American sex revolution discussed. We do not have sufficient evidence of strictly anatomical and physiological changes directly and indirectly related to sex activity which would explain the increased motivating power of the sex drive. But we do have sufficient proof of a disinhibition of sex drive from the controls of the restraining psychosocial factor-values. The force of many religious, moral, aesthetic and social values that taboo all the prenuptial and extramarital sex relations has been progressively weakened during the last few centuries, and the last few decades especially. And many of these inhibitive values have been replaced by the values that commend and recommend a more free satisfaction of sex passion. . . .

Changing Standards

While the Ideational [religious, moral] values tend to restrain unlawful sex activities, the Sensate [secular] values aim to disinhibit and approve them. At their present disintegrating stage the Sensate values tend to approve potentially an unrestrained sex freedom, and recommend the fullest possible satisfaction of sex love in all its forms. This basic change in psychosocial factors has manifested itself in revaluation of the previous standards by modern American (and Western) men and women. The sex drive is now declared to be the most vital mainspring of human behavior. In the name of science, its fullest satisfaction is urged as a necessary condition of man's health and happiness. Sex inhibitions are viewed as the main source of frustrations, mental and physical illness and criminality. Sexual chastity is ridiculed as a prudish superstition. Nuptial loyalty is stigmatized as an antiquated hypocrisy. Father is painted as a jealous tyrant desirous of castrating his sons to prevent incest with their mother. Motherhood is interpreted as a "mommism," wrecking the lives of children. Sons and daughters are depicted as filled with the "complexes" of seduction of their mother and father, respectively. Sexual profligacy and prowess are proudly glamorized. *Homo sapiens* is replaced by *homo sexualis* packed with genital, anal, oral, and cutaneous libidos. The traditional "child of God" created in God's image is turned into a sexual apparatus powered by sex instinct, pre-occupied with sex matters, aspiring for, and dreaming and thinking mainly of, sex relations. Sexualization of human beings has about reached its saturation point. Such in black and white has been the psychosocial change of the modern man's mentality, aspirations, emotions, and values paralleling the sexual revolution in his behavior.

Effect on the Culture

If the mind, behavior, and values of contemporary men and women have been notably sexualized, similar sexualization of our entire culture and of every social institution must be expected. And if this is so, then the depth and extent of the current sex revolution must be incomparably more than a mere change in the personality and conduct of our contemporaries. . . .

Sexually Frank Literature

In its topics, personages, scenes, and aims, our literature is largely centered on sex, especially its pathological forms. . . .

Almost all eminent American writers of the last fifty years,—[Theodore] Dreiser, [Sinclair] Lewis, [Eugene] O'Neill, [Ernest] Hemingway, [William] Faulkner, [John] Steinbeck, [James T.] Farrell,—and a legion of less notable ones have paid their tribute to sex, either by making it the main topic of many of their works, or, what is perhaps more symptomatic, by devoting to it much attention in works supposedly dealing with problems quite different. In books of this latter sort, sex topics could easily have been omitted; yet erotic scenes are painted onto each canvas, whether of the Spanish Civil War [Hemingway], of the migration of Okies [Faulkner], or of the Southern Jukes and Kallikaks [pseudonyms of families studied to prove genetic causes for criminality and feeblemindedness].

What is even more significant, many of these authors display the erotic excesses and disloyalties of their characters as perfectly normal. Whereas the great writers of the nineteenth century, like [Leo] Tolstoy and [Gustave] Flaubert, depicted illicit passion as a tragedy for which hero and heroine alike paid with their lives or by long suffering, most of the adulteries and other sins treated in contemporary literature are considered by the authors enjoyable adventures in the monotonous existence of modern men and women. Sometimes such illicit relationships are described as a commendable liberation from the antiquated marriage bonds. At other times they are considered hygienic actions freeing individuals from their repressions, psychoneurosis, and other mental disorders. Not infrequently they are heralded as harbingers of a "higher" form of companionate marriage. Rarely, if ever, are they condemned as a dangerous disease. By such treatment, modern literature disinhibits rather than wisely restrains lust. It undermines rather than vitalizes marriage and the family. It weakens rather than reinforces the control of animal propensities by man's higher self. In all these respects, it demoralizes rather than integrates the total personality.

Pulp Literature as Pornography

When we turn to the sham literature of today, we find an atmosphere even more saturated by sex. For in this pulp writing, sexualization has gone much farther, and has assumed much uglier forms than in the serious literature. The sham literature of our age is designed for the commercial cultivation, propagation, and exploitation of the most degraded forms of behavior. It is pornography that appeals to the basest propensities of that "worst of the beast", as the demoralized human animal was named by Plato and Aristotle. The world of this popular literature is a sort of human zoo, inhabited by raped, mutilated, and murdered females, and by he-males outmatching in beastiality any caveman and out-lusting the lustiest of animals; male and female alike are hardened in cynical contempt of human life and values. And what is especially symptomatic is that many of these human animals are made to seem to luxuriate in this way of life, just as, we must assume, the readers enjoy it. This cheap Dante's inferno of aphrodisiacs is painted in the most captivating colors. Instead of exhibiting its filth and rottenness, the pulp-sexualists daze the reader with the glamor of "smartness", "orgasmic" curves, "dynamic" lines, violent passions, and "freedom unlimited" to do anything one wants to do.

Giving detailed descriptions of various techniques of sexual approach, and vivid scenes of kissing, embracing, and copulating, and while brutally dramatizing rape and other sexual perversions, this pornographically illustrated pulp-literature demoralizes and dehumanizes millions of readers. Its audience, as well as its quantity, is incomparably larger than that of serious literature. This pulp stuff is poured onto the market in hundreds of thousands of copies of dime and quarter novels, in millions of copies of various magazines, in many millions of erotic comics and periodical stories. The sadistic novels of Mickey Spillane have sold more than 25 million copies! The total output of this sort of stuff is to be counted in the hundreds of millions. In addition, some of this material is turned into popular movies, is brought into millions of homes by radio and television, and is even dramatized on the legitimate stage. All in all, this stuff has become omnipresent in our lives, and everyone of us is incessantly and increasingly exposed to its deadly radiations.

Large-scale manufacture and commercial exploitation of these sex-saturated books would not be possible if they did not appeal to the common literary tastes of millions. Whether we like it or not, the obsession with sex in our literature is an ugly fact beyond reasonable doubt. . . .

Music

The trend of sexualization has particularly manifested itself in the semi-popular and popular music of our time. Here indeed the theme has become striking. If it is still somewhat tempered in such shows as *Oklahoma, South Pacific, Kiss Me Kate, Kismet* and *My Fair Lady,* it has become naked, seductive and abductive, lusty and perverse in popular jazz and song hits and in the bulk of night club, television and radio music. References to kissing, embracing, and going to bed are essential to their lyrics. The songs are monotonously chanted by voiceless crooners innocent of the art of *bel-canto* [a musical form emphasizing beautiful singing over the meaning of the words]. Their bleating is underscored by their gyrations, contortions, and bodily rhythms all too dear in sexual innuendo and undisguised meaning. Records of this sort of "music" are sold by the millions and their nauseous repetition occupies the lion's share of radio and television programs. The composers and crooners of these "hits" are idolized by millions, and are financially remunerated many times more amply than are the composers of the serious music of today. . . .

Passive Reactions

As a nation we are usually quite alert to the dangers threatening our well-being. We notice their early symptoms in time, and promptly take the necessary countermeasures.

Our listless drift towards sex anarchy seems to be an exception to this rule. Aside from a few old-fashioned voices crying in the wilderness, no alarms are sounded by the nation's leaders in the press or over radio or television. On our lifeways, no posters warn us with: "Danger! Slow Down! Sex Anarchy Ahead!" No nationwide educational campaign brings home to our citizens the grim consequences of an overdeveloped sex freedom. No big drive has been launched to combat promiscuity, premarital and extramarital relations, divorce, and desertion.

Still less attention is paid to the progressive sexualization of our culture, institutions, and way of life. We often spend vast amounts of money, energy, and time, in fighting various social maladies, yet we do little to stop any further increase of sex freedom. We do not tolerate excessively dangerous political, social, or economic anarchy, yet we seem to be tolerant of sex disorders.

The Necessity of Resistance

Does our apathy in this matter mean that we are unaware of the drift? Or does it signify our approval of the growing sex obsession, an acceptance of it as another step toward a fuller freedom and a happier life? Or, perhaps, does it represent a symptom of our incapacity to free ourselves from deep addiction to promiscuity?

If we are unaware of the real situation, it is high time we awakened from our ignorance. If we have lost the capacity to resist, it is urgent that we regain it. If we expect blessings from sex anarchy, it is vital that we cast aside this foolishness and look soberly at the sorry state of affairs. For there is a dangerous hue of serious trouble on the horizon. Our sex freedom is beginning to expand beyond the limits of safety, beginning to degenerate into anarchy.

The Consequences

[Sex freedom has caused] a rapid increase of divorce, desertion, and separation, and of premarital and extramarital relations, with the boundary between lawful marriage and illicit liaisons tending to become more and more tenuous. Still greater has been the deterioration of the family as a union of parents and children, with "fluid marriages" producing a super-abundance of the physically, morally, and mentally defective children, or no children at all.

As a consequence, in spite of our still developing economic prosperity, and our outstanding progress in science and technology, in education, in medical care; notwithstanding our democratic regime and way of life, and our modern methods of social service; in brief, in spite of the innumerable and highly effective techniques and agencies for social improvement, there has been no decrease in adult criminality, juvenile delinquency, and mental disease, no lessening of the sense of insecurity and of frustration. If anything, these have been on the increase, and already have become the major problems of our nation. What this means is that the poisonous fruits of our sex-marriage-family relationships are contaminating our social life and our cultural and personal well-being. They have already passed beyond the phase of being possibly dangerous, and have become ugly and deadly realities as solid and certain as any facts can be.

Our trend toward sex anarchy has not yet produced catastrophic consequences. Nevertheless, the first syndromes of grave disease have already appeared.

Reclaiming the Ideals of the Sexual Revolution

Judith Levine

*As America approached the end of the twentieth century, the
AIDS epidemic contributed to a culture of fear that in turn encouraged a return to more conservative sexual values. The teaching of abstinence to young people became increasingly prevalent,
especially in response to issues of teen pregnancy. The single life
had been depicted as ideal by proponents of the sexual revolution. In the late eighties, however, being single was often viewed
as a trap one escaped through the monogamy of marriage. While
the sexual revolution had characterized free love as a key to a
more enlightened existence, by the 1990s sex was becoming a
highly restricted activity, and the punishment for a liberal sex
life was AIDS.*

*In the following article Judith Levine voices her resistance to
the fear and conservatism surrounding sex in the late twentieth
century. She argues that sex is an unworthy scapegoat for what
conservatives call a decline in moral values. She feels that AIDS
is used to instill a fear that causes society to forget the positive
lessons of the sexual revolution. Above all, Levine contends that
the vilification of sex only results in driving people farther apart.
Levine is a journalist whose writing focuses on sex, gender, and
families. She is the founder of the feminist group* No More Nice
Girls *and is the author of* My Enemy, My Love: Women, Men,
and the Dilemmas of Gender *and* Harmful to Minors: The
Perils of Protecting Children from Sex.

In the past decade [1978 to 1988] we've witnessed sex the
question transformed into sex the problem. The problem of
teenage pregnancy has become the problem of teenage sex, so

Judith Levine, "Thinking About Sex," *Tikkun,* March/April 1988, pp. 43–45. Copyright
© 1988 by the Institute for Labor and Mental Health. Reproduced by permission of
Tikkun: A Bimonthly Jewish Critique of Politics, Culture & Society.

we try to teach abstinence instead of contraception and convince ourselves that teenagers have sex only because of peer pressure. AIDS is perceived not as a horrible disease of the body, but as the wasting away of the morals of the body politic. The cure is to contain, not the virus, but nonconventional, nonmonogamous sex.

But you don't have to travel far rightward to discover such attitudes. The middle is rife with them, too. No presidential candidate is unqualifiedly prochoice. No Congress member objects when [conservative former North Carolina senator] Jesse Helms fulminates on the Senate floor about "safe sodomy." [Journalist and social commentator] Bill Moyers speculates that promiscuity—too many undisciplined young cocks strutting around the inner city's roosts—is the cause of the black family's dissolution. [Civil rights leader] Jesse Jackson, instead of refuting him, drops his economic analysis and preaches a return to the church and its sexual morality. Recently, on NBC's "Scared Sexless," host Connie Chung reacts quizzically to Education Secretary William Bennett's remark that "AIDS may give us an opportunity to discourage [sex], and that might be a good thing." But she concludes that, plagues or no, less sex is better, especially for teenagers. She doesn't say why.

Losing Sight of the Sexual Revolution

In response to all this, the left says nothing. In fact, it consistently puts sex at the bottom of the agenda (my mother has been fighting with my father, both of them old leftists, for forty years about the political centrality of abortion) or demonstrates downright antisex and antipleasure biases. In the 1980s, ever more squeamish about appearing unserious, it distances itself from popular culture (which is all about fun) and from prosex feminists, gays, and other erotic minorities for whom sexual freedom is a fundamental struggle. This is more than an abstract problem: according to the Centers for Disease Control, in the 1990s AIDS may kill more Americans annually than were lost during the entire Vietnam War, yet no left group makes the epidemic a forefront issue.

Meanwhile, progressives dismiss the Sexual Revolution as a childish flight of caprice, and though they don't see AIDS as the scourge of God, they use the disease as a justification for endorsing certain kinds of sex and relationships and censuring others. Not as coldhearted as Bennett, but equally insulting to the people dying, these "progressives" find in AIDS the silver lining of newly "meaningful," committed sex. Even from the gay community a pious monogamism emanates—*vis* the mass marriage ceremony at the gay and lesbian march on Washington.

Fading Feminism

As for feminists, a small rowdy band of prosex guerrillas like No More Nice Girls carries the flame of women's sexual freedom, but all around them the flame dims to a flicker. Influential moderates like Betty Friedan eschew public discourses on lesbianism and sex as "exhibitionist," and steer activism elsewhere. In the early 1980s, abortion is suddenly a "family" issue, and a secondary one at that. If there were good daycare and socialized medicine, the argument runs, we'd all want children, and the demand for abortion would disappear. Lately, abortion finds itself nestling under the antiseptic rubric of "reproductive freedom," with forced caesareans, *in vitro* fertilization, surrogacy, and other politics of modern motherhood. It's as if sex—which, if I'm not mistaken, is the cause of pregnancy—had nothing to do with it. In fact, the feminists most consistently passionate about c—ks and c—ts are Women Against Pornography—and they would wash my mouth out with soap for saying it!

Reclaiming the Revolution

All this distresses me mightily. . . . I consider pleasure a revolutionary goal. And I still endorse the commitment of the

Sexual Revolution and the early women's movement to forging new personal alliances, new forms of love and friendship—including sexual ones. Though never a smash-monogamy zealot, I believe in destabilizing traditional sexual setups and struggling, as we did in the 1960s and 1970s, with the emotions that go with such a cultural upheaval.

At the risk of sounding "nostalgic," or, in the age of AIDS, either frivolous or mad, I contend that we can't change society if we don't challenge the sexual hegemony of the nuclear family and resist its enforcement of adult heterosexual monogamy and its policing of all other forms of sexuality within it and outside it. Supporting "alternative" families or giving lip service to gay rights isn't enough; we must militantly stand up for everybody whose sexuality falls outside "acceptable" bourgeois arrangements—even far outside of them.

But you can't do this without asking fundamental questions about sex. Questions like, is monogamy better? (My answer: not necessarily.) What's wrong with kids having sex? (Often, nothing.) Why is it worse to pay for sex than to pay for someone to listen to your intimate problems or care for your infant? (You tell me.) You can't ask those questions if you whisk sexuality to the bottom of the list of "serious issues" after peace, or childcare, or even AIDS.

Challenging Monogamy

Indeed, AIDS should have us thinking harder than ever about how to preserve pleasure in our lives. If the disease limits our options, at the very least we don't have to be sanctimonious about it! I may currently like having sex with only one person, but I don't like feeling I'd better sleep with him exclusively from now on, or death will us part. Fear of death is about as felicitous a motivation for monogamy as fear of impoverishment is for staying married.

We shouldn't be looking for meaning in sex at all, in fact, but rather trying to strip implicit meaning from sex. I don't mean pushing for casual sex, but allowing a separation of sex from commitment and then, by conscious decision only, rejoining the two. This would not only emancipate women to make the choices men have always made about what sex means in a given relationship, it would enhance the possibility for stronger alliances, both passionate and emotional.

Relationships as More than Sex

In thinking about how that could be done, I recall a 1983 piece by Edmund White, "Paradise Found," about his circle of gay friends and lovers. Outside the rules and expectations of family, relationships were highly fluid. Unlike heterosexual couples, who date, become monogamous, marry, integrate into one another's families, have children, and adjust their sex lives accordingly, a gay lover could be anything from a trick to a husband, or over time, both. Though radical gayness singled out sexuality as an essence of identity, it also freed relationships from being defined by sex. In the novel *Dancing in the Dark,* Janet Hobhouse described "these loving friends, admitted into their [early Renaissance painter] Giotto heaven one by one as each 'came out' and professed the faith, free to touch and kiss like angels. . . ." If the meanings of sex were myriad, the use of sex was plain: pleasure.

Using the Lessons of the Revolution

Our task today is not to pine away in nostalgia, but neither is it to disavow the sexual liberation we fought for in the past decades. We need to keep pleasure as a vital part of the progressive vision at the same time as we confront AIDS, which vanquishes pleasure more powerfully than any repression the right or the left could ever dream up. We must help our children feel that sex is good in an era when sex can bring death, and learn how to relate sexually to each other when new relationships are short-circuited, and old ones sustained, by fear.

The first priority (and it's sickening that this doesn't go without saying) must be a unified fight against AIDS. We must demand government funds for research, medical treatment, and education, and oppose repressive policies on testing, employment, housing, and schooling. And since AIDS is becoming a disease of the poor and drug-addicted, we must redouble our efforts to eradicate poverty.

Combating AIDS with Reality

We have no choice but to teach children safe sex, but we must avoid hysteria, too. If a boy is gay, he is at high risk, but politicized awareness of his identity is his best defense. Vigorous education in the gay community has stabilized the spread of AIDS there. A lesbian child is virtually risk-free. Only one case of "apparent" female-to-female transmission has been reported. Now the media are sounding the alarm about heterosexual transmission—and indeed it is rising. Still, by far the most likely heterosexual carriers are poor, black, or Hispanic IV drug users and their partners; the most sensible AIDS-prevention technique, then, is to give kids real reasons and resources to stay away from serious drugs and away from sexual relations with people who use them. Excluding drug users, only four percent of people with AIDS are heterosexual. We are all fearful enough about sex; there's no point exaggerating the danger.

Educating Youth

Nobody should make assumptions about what kids know about sex. Research shows that while they're highly aware of sex generally, they're often pretty ignorant about the details. Good sex education is safe sex education too. Helping kids to be aware of their bodies—of health and contraception, masturbation, sensual touching, and fantasy as well as intercourse—and of their feelings about sexuality can only make them better able to practice safe and egalitarian sex in what could be history's most honest chapter of sexual relations.

Sexual behavior, moreover, should never be governed by a separate category of morality. If we want our kids to balance

111

their own desires with responsibility and consideration for others, to express their needs and objections freely but cooperate within a community, then we should practice and teach our kids these values in sex, too. Teaching abstinence as "right" is not only puritanical and ineffective in limiting sexual activity, but it fuels prejudice against people whose sexual expression may be more flagrant, and it implies that disease is a punishment for sin.

Resisting the Fear of AIDS

AIDS presents one of the biggest challenges in history to our survival as a loving community. Both safety and compassion require us to stop seeing those we've been taught to revile as the Other. When we are ruled by fear and alienation, it is easy for extreme attitudes and repressive policies to start sounding reasonable. On the day of the 1987 gay march in Washington, D.C., for instance, the *New York Post*'s lead story, headlined AIDS MONSTER, stereotyped the classic diseased and depraved homosexual, hunted by police for molesting what seemed like countless boys. It is easy to see through the *Post*'s bigotry, but the story plays on the same assumption that supports mandatory testing and disclosure: that people with AIDS lie, remain selfishly ignorant, and deliberately infect—murder—others, so desperate and devoid of social responsibility are they. When "they" are so unlike "us," Draconian measures like tattooing or quarantine seem necessary "for the greater good." In reality, the greater good demands reaching deep to find our human similarities and also respecting our sexual differences.

Saying Yes to Sex

The antisex hysteria of the 1980s also presents a great challenge to us as lovers. Fear and malaise are counter-aphrodisiac (the number one complaint sex therapists hear is lack of desire). We need not exacerbate them with self-righteousness.

Married people, who these days seem to have no sensual outlet besides stroking Baby's cheek and watching the VCR, go around gloating about their maturity and security. Single people are home watching their VCR, too—and watching their backs. With movies like *Fatal Attraction,* it's no wonder. Once envied, singles are now blamed; once considered free, they're now portrayed as trapped.

Where can we look for prosex messages in the AIDS era? I found one in the most threatened quarter, the gay community, in the educational comic books distributed by the Gay Men's Health Crisis. These depict sexual types from leathermen to clones . . . having phone sex, masturbating, or role-playing, all with minimum risk and maximum heat. Explicitly, humorously sexual, indeed happily pornographic, these pamphlets are pragmatic: they meet their constituency where it lives and do not try to preach living differently. But they imply more— that it's unnecessary to foment aversion to sex through moralizing or hyperbolizing. Death is aversion enough. It's driven many back into the closet and made celibates of countless more.

Instead, the lascivious comic-book hunks are saying: affirm sex. While death is all around us, let us nurture pleasure—for pleasure is life. Even now, especially now, just say yes.

Women's Mixed Reactions to the Sexual Revolution

Linda Wolfe

The sexual revolution is generally recognized as a product of the 1960s and 70s. By the 1980s, America's sexual attitudes were moving in different—and even more divergent—directions. While the music and film industry were saturated with sexual overtones and increases in premarital sex had been clearly documented, the advent of the AIDS crisis swept the country with fear and a call for safer sex. The women's movement paid increased attention to issues such as date rape and pornography. In short, sexual attitudes were as diverse and conflicting as ever.

In 1981 Cosmopolitan *magazine (with a circulation of 1.5 million at the time) conducted a massive survey of its readers, asking them to share their feelings about the sexual revolution of the past two decades and what changes, positive or negative, it had brought about. The magazine was intended to appeal to attractive, intelligent and aware women between eighteen and thirty-five. The editor of* Cosmopolitan, *Helen Gurley Brown (author of* Sex and the Single Girl*), promoted an image of a sophisticated and sexually liberated woman. Thus, it is surprising that* Cosmopolitan's *readers had mixed reactions to the sexual revolution. Only half of the respondents felt that the sexual revolution had had a positive effect on the lives of women. Linda Wolfe, the author of the following article that reports the views of respondents to the* Cosmopolitan *survey, is a journalist and novelist who wrote the Edgar Award–nominated book* Wasted.

*M*ajor findings:

Forty-nine percent of the respondents felt that the sexual revolution had had a good effect on the lives of most women. Fifty-three percent felt that it had caused sex to be too casual or made it hard for them to find acceptable reasons to say no to a man sexually. (The figures add to more than 100 percent because 2 percent of the women straddled both sides of the question.)

As a group, the *Cosmo* women are perhaps the most sexually experienced women in western history. They tend to start their erotic lives young, have sex with a considerable number of partners, and practice a considerable variety of sexual techniques. They are comfortable about acknowledging masturbation and sexual fantasy, and the great majority of them believe that good sex is possible without love. These women have apparently reaped the sexual fruits planted by idealistic social reformers throughout the eighteenth, nineteenth and early twentieth centuries. But as the figures above show, by no means all the *Cosmo* women are happy about the harvest.

Dissatisfied with the Revolution

More than half of them are disappointed in or disillusioned with the sexual revolution.

Why? Is their dissatisfaction simply a result of the usual human tendency to disparage whatever exists and long for the greener grass of whatever does not? Or are there, in fact, real and serious flaws in the sexual revolution, at least as it affects women? The *Cosmo* women who were dissatisfied with the sexual revolution seemed to feel there were. Many believed that, like the heirs to political revolutions, they had been betrayed. They had participated in the overthrow of one tyranny only to see another installed in its place. A 24-year-old schoolteacher from Pennsylvania was typical of this group:

> The sexual revolution is in reality a big sad joke that we women mindlessly allowed to be played on us. What we did when we freed ourselves physically was free men to live out their wildest fantasies of promiscuity and irresponsibility. Men never wanted to form commitments, but in the past

they had to in order to obtain sex. Now that we women are no longer afraid of one-night stands, men don't have to commit themselves. Before the revolution, life offered the average women half a glass with which to slake her thirst. Now she's being doused with a fire hose.

Similarly, a 24-year-old aeronautics worker from Florida wrote:

I have to say that the sexual revolution has made sex worse for me, not better. Yes, the men I meet know how to kiss, suck, touch and fondle. But they do it to satisfy their own egos, not because they want to give me pleasure. They don't really care about me, about women, just about sex and their egos. In the past a man used to have to offer a relationship in order to get sex. . . . But now, since so many women give sex so freely, the men offer nothing—and we women must accept this, even if we don't like it. Throughout the centuries, women have gotten the short end of the stick. We're still getting it. Only now it's a different stick.

A Male Revolution?

The feeling that sexual freedom had benefited men more than women was the predominant underlying complaint against the sexual revolution. The dissatisfied women did not register this complaint out of a Victorian sensibility; they did not argue that sex was not as physically pleasurable to women as it was to men. Rather, they tended to feel that what women wanted from enjoyable sex was not what men wanted from it.

What women wanted, said the critics of the sexual revolution, was not necessarily love. Three-fourths of the *Cosmo* women, including a large number of those who disliked the sexual revolution, believed that good sex was possible without love. What they wanted, *needed,* said the critics, was some form of committed ongoing interchange, and men did not. They believed, for example, that men, unlike women, thoroughly enjoyed one-night stands.

I wonder about this distinction. If it were true, why would so many millions of men continue to opt, today, for living-together arrangements and even marriage? (Despite the sexual revolution and divorce rate, the latest census shows no decline in the American marriage rate.) Some men may have one-night stands—isolated sexual encounters after which they never call again—not so much because they like casual sex as because they decide, after an evening with a particular woman, that they don't care to pursue further intimacy with *her*. What woman doesn't have a friend who complained about having sex with some man who never called her again and then learned, six months or a year later, that he was about to marry someone else—thereby throwing cold water on her theory that he was a devotee of casual sex?

Sex Without Commitment

Of course, there *are* men who never form commitments, who never have sex with the same woman twice if they can help it. And although I suspect they are rarer than some imagine, to the woman who has been unable to link up with a lover willing to form an ongoing relationship with her, the sexual revolution can seem empty indeed. A 23-year-old from New York City writes:

> I'm always surprised when I hear from a man after we've spent the night in bed. You can't count on it. That's the way men are. And we women, myself included, have made fools of ourselves by going along with the sexual revolution. We've made it possible for them to have sex with us at the drop of a hat, and never feel enough responsibility to call up the next day and see how we are, or even *if* we are. There are nights I say goodbye to a lover to whom I've just given the greatest ecstasies in bed, and I think to myself, Here I am in my dangerous Greenwich Village apartment, with its fire escapes and dingy staircases. Maybe someone will break in and rape me during the night. Or kill me. Will this guy I'm saying goodbye to ever wonder about me in the morning? Will he wonder enough to call and discover I don't answer

the phone? Will he notify the police? Probably not. That's the sexual revolution for you.

Pressures of the Revolution

Some women who were dissatisfied with the sexual revolution felt that a great deal of what they said and did sexually was insincere. They pretended to enjoyments they did not actually feel. A 22-year-old from Maine was typical:

> I feel 40, I've had so many lovers. I usually go to bed with men on the first date. All the guys I meet expect this. If you don't do it, you run the very high risk of never seeing them again. I try to convince myself I enjoy sex with a total, or semi-total, stranger. I do it because the guys I meet are convinced that they do. But I really detest it. Why can't things be the way they used to be before this sexual revolution? Why can't a woman get to know and like a guy first, and then have intercourse with him?

And a 19-year-old from Oregon who pretends to an enjoyment of sadomasochistic sex with her lover, but who has never had an orgasm during this kind of sex, writes:

> My feelings about the sexual revolution are that it is moving too fast. People are too free about sex. But you have to act like you like it or you'll be sitting home all alone.

A Believer in the Revolution

Those who approve of and admire the sexual revolution do not feel they have been insincere about their pleasures. And, usually, they are women who have had, at least from time to time, ongoing committed relationships with men. A 22-year-old woman from Oregon . . . is typical: Although she had some ten lovers during college, many of whom were one-night stands, she praises the sexual revolution because it enabled her to experiment with men until she found the one she has now, a man she is planning to marry at the end of the year:

My earlier sexual experiences, while not very good, helped me over some insecurities and feelings of unattractiveness, and paved the way for me to enjoy my present boyfriend. I am all for the sexual revolution. There are some problems connected with it, but for the most part it seems to mature people faster and help them not to have fears about sexual feelings. Life seems a lot more natural this way.

Different Things to Different People

The contrast between the feelings of this Oregon woman and those of the Oregon woman whose letter precedes hers suggests an all-important . . . if not surprising . . . fact about the sexual revolution: It is different things to different people. To one woman, the revolution may be in her having had premarital sex with one or two lovers. To another, it may be in her having had a dozen. To one woman, it means she can comfortably discuss with her husband the sexual techniques most likely to bring her to orgasm. To another it's that the men who call her expect her to accompany them to orgies. There has been a sexual revolution, but when people say they are for it or against it, they are often speaking about very different phenomena.

So it is not enough to know that a woman approves of the sexual revolution for Reason X, or disapproves of it for Reason Y. For her reasons to be meaningful, one needs to know what experiences shaped her reasoning. Is her sexual revolution the same as yours or mine?

The Sexual Revolution's Effects on the American Family

Elizabeth Fox-Genovese

In the following selection Elizabeth Fox-Genovese describes the changes in the American family since the end of World War II. Both economic and social factors have contributed to the decline of stable, two-parent families, she writes. Specifically, economic changes now require most women to work outside of the home. In addition, the sexual revolution has severed the link between sexuality and morality, thus making out-of-wedlock birth more socially acceptable. Feminists have lauded these developments as essential to women's liberation. However, despite these changes, Fox-Genovese insists that most Americans remain committed to traditional moral and family values. She calls for a return to public morality that directly contradicts the sexual revolution's advocacy of sexual openness and freedom. Fox-Genovese is a professor of history and the humanities at Emory University and the author of the books Feminism Without Illusions: A Critique of Individualism *and* Feminism Is Not the Story of My Life: How the Feminist Elite Has Lost Touch with the Real Concerns of Women.

As we face the third millennium, it is hard to doubt that the American family is in disarray. Divorce claims more than half of all marriages and more than one-third of all children are born to single mothers. Signaling the revolution in attitudes toward the importance of traditional family bonds, the words "adultery" and "illegitimacy" have effectively disappeared from our vocabulary. Increasingly children, even those with two resident parents, are left to their own devices, which, the frightening statistics tell us, too frequently lead them to

Elizabeth Fox-Genovese, "The National Prospect: A Symposium," *Commentary,* vol. 100, November 1995, pp. 53–54. Copyright © 1995 by the American Jewish Committee. All rights reserved. Reproduced by permission of the publisher and the author.

crime, drug addiction, alcoholism, suicide, and violent death. The world of stable, two-parent families and protected childhoods to which Americans turned with such enthusiasm in 1945 seems gone beyond recall.

In retrospect, the serenity of attitudes and the stability of institutions that prevailed in 1945 may be seen more as wish than as reality, for the forces that would shortly transform the United States almost beyond recognition were already pulling at the leash. Nineteen forty-five did not so much inaugurate a return to normality as the first glimmerings of an unprecedented dual revolution in economics and sexuality. That dual revolution radically transformed Americans' attitudes and expectations about women's roles and family dynamics, but, radical pronouncements to the contrary notwithstanding, it did not shake most Americans' commitment to stable families and responsible child-rearing. What it did do was make the realization of both increasingly difficult.

Severing the Link Between Sex and Morality

The sexual revolution broke upon popular consciousness in the mid- to late 1960's and, by the early 1970's, carried the day. In 1969, two out of every three Americans disapproved of premarital sex. Four short years later, in 1973, only 48 percent disapproved, and 43 percent believed that premarital sex was OK. In retrospect, it seems clear that most Americans supported the sexual revolution because they thought that it freed "nice" girls to have sex before marriage without ruining their reputations. It apparently never occurred to them that this small relaxation in sexual "morality" would permanently sever the link between sex and morality, making it increasingly difficult to censor any sexual behavior at all.

Thus, what initially looked like a minor adjustment in courting conventions rapidly led to open marriage, single motherhood, an explosion of pornography, the celebration of "man-boy" love, X-rated films around the corner and on television, and any other shattering of taboos that human appetites could devise.

Feminism has ridden the crest of the sexual revolution, insisting upon sexual freedom as the bedrock of women's liberation. For many feminists, the consolidation of this freedom has required not merely the constitutional guarantee of a woman's "right" to abortion, but also women's freedom from the control of men through families, specifically no-fault divorce and public acceptance (not to mention financial support) of single motherhood. Thus, even while some feminists deplore pornography as yet another manifestation of men's brutality against women, few if any have been willing to advocate a curtailment of the sexual revolution in the name of morality.

Women's Changing Domestic Roles

Not for nothing have feminists insisted that those who evoke morality and family values more often than not favor women's return to the traditional domestic roles of the immediate postwar era when American families were catching up on the childbearing they had deferred during the Great Depression. Determined to consolidate women's massive entry into the labor force, not to mention their personal freedom, feminists easily confuse any mention of morality with men's determination to confine women to the bedroom and the kitchen.

As it happens, however, the economic revolution that intertwined with the sexual revolution of the late 1960's and early 1970's has made such a restoration impossible. In the 1990's, most working women work because they must. And most work throughout much if not all of their childbearing years. Today, the typical working woman is a mother or likely to become one, and the typical mother is a working woman. Ordinary Americans, whose families depend upon women's earnings, live intimately with that necessity, which they do not confuse with an evasion of moral responsibility.

By the same token, the recognition that most women must work does not lead most Americans to a devil-take-the-hindmost attitude toward morality. To the contrary, almost two-thirds (according to a recent survey reported in the *Wall Street Journal*) regard the collapse of morality as our most pressing national concern. Yet slightly more than two-thirds do not merely accept the necessity for wives to work, they approve of their doing so. And to complicate the picture further, the majority of American women continue to view marriage and children as essential ingredients in their ideal life, just as they continue strongly to support—and practice—marital fidelity.

Trying to Maintain Family Values

These attitudes make it difficult to argue that most American women regard traditional commitments to a husband and children—what most of us would call the bedrock of family values—as just another form of male oppression from which they must be liberated. Many Americans, in other words, are doing their best to practice both family values and morality, which challenges us to explain the widespread perception that both families and morality are in disarray.

Only the arrogant or the stupid could pretend to offer a simple explanation of the gap between practice and perception, but some things are clear. We are all, good intentions to the contrary notwithstanding, failing our children, and we are failing them because neither public nor private solutions to their problems will alone suffice. Most families cannot do the job without some assistance and encouragement, and the public sector demonstrably cannot replace families, or even compensate for the absence of one parent. Well beyond infancy, children require and deserve sustained attention from both a mother and a father.

Advocating a Return to Public Morality

But if our policies are failing our children, our public pronouncements are failing them even worse. For one major consequence of the sexual revolution's divorce of sexuality from morality has been the ensuing divorce of reproduction from morality. Willy-nilly, we have conspired to transform the moral work of society, notably responsibility for the next generation, into servants' work which none should be coerced to perform. Worse, we have beaten an unseemly retreat from the authority of moral obligation, thereby reducing the fulfillment of moral obligation to a matter of personal choice.

Whether we count ourselves among those who would liberate women from responsibility to children or those who would impose that responsibility upon them, we are ending in the same disastrous impasse, namely, the privatization of morality which, if it is to deserve its name, must be both public and binding, and which, if it is to command allegiance, must take account of a world in which most good mothers must work.

The Sexual Revolution Should Not Be Abandoned

Scott Stossel

Many people associate the beginning of the sexual revolution with the introduction of the birth control pill in 1960 and the end of the revolution with the 1981 onset of the AIDS crisis. There is no doubt that AIDS created a tremendous fear in sexually active Americans, which caused a conservative backlash to the sexual revolution. However, many people believe that a liberal reaction to that backlash has already occurred. In the following article Scott Stossel acknowledges the fact that the sexual revolution has led to increased occurrences of sexually transmitted diseases. Nevertheless, Stossel asserts that the sexual revolution led to many liberal social and political changes that should not be abandoned, such as increased rights for women and gays. Stossel is a senior editor at the Atlantic Monthly *magazine. He has written articles on subjects as diverse as politics, publishing, the war on terror, and sports.*

During the 1984 primary [election] season, Ronald Reagan worried publicly that Americans were having too much sex. Promiscuity, he lamented, had become "acceptable, even stylish." The very word "promiscuity," with its reproachful moral overtones, had been replaced by the more accepting term "sexually active." What had once been "a sacred expression of love," had become "casual and cheap." The country's moral fabric was fraying dangerously. Who had set us on this road to Sodom? Liberals.

Accusations like Reagan's do not necessarily presume that liberals are friskier than other people—believe it or not, one study actually found that the very conservative are 10 percent

Scott Stossel, "The Sexual Counterrevolution," *The American Prospect,* vol. 33, July/ August 1997, pp. 74–83. Copyright © 1997 by The American Prospect, Inc., 11 Beacon St., Suite 1120, Boston, MA 02108. All rights reserved. Reproduced by permission.

more likely than the very liberal to be conducting extramarital affairs and three times more likely than the very liberal and the moderate to find sadomasochism an acceptable practice. Rather, Reagan's comments represent a typical version of the traditional conservative's interpretation of the "sexual revolution": It was part of the sinful sixties-seventies counterculture; it was a weakening of morals caused by trends and policies, such as wider availability of contraceptives and broader acceptance of premarital sex, that liberals advocated; and it was bad.

Liberals and Conservatives Clash

The sexual revolution is clearly one of those ideological battlegrounds—like the conflicts over college curricula, abortion, and "the sixties"—where liberals and conservatives clash over culture, politics, and religion simultaneously. Many liberals would insist—rightly—that the sexual revolution helped bring about changes for the better: broader rights for gays and women, wider use of contraceptives, acceptance of premarital cohabitation. Many conservatives would insist—also rightly— that the sexual revolution undermined traditional social and religious bonds and that this loosening of mores caused an explosion of sexually transmitted diseases (STDs). Conservatives have used the epidemics of AIDS and other STDs to re-energize their traditional moral arguments against sex outside marriage. Liberals, on the other hand, still champion what they consider to be the revolution's moral gains; they advocate improving contraceptive availability and sex education to preserve these gains while fighting disease and raising awareness.

Today we live with what many people believe—despite some studies showing sexual activity today to be as promiscuous as, if not more promiscuous than, at the height of the revolution—is a counterrevolution ushered in by AIDS. But is this backlash against the revolution a reality? What is the connection between public morality and public health? And who has more authority to speak on these issues: liberals advocating sex education and public health, or conservatives advocating abstinence and self-discipline?

On May 10, 1960, the Food and Drug Administration (FDA) announced the approval of a new drug produced by G.D. Searle & Company, called Enovid. Some 21 years later, on June 5, 1981, *Morbidity and Mortality Weekly* reported the appearance of a strange new pneumonia in five otherwise healthy gay men. On neither day were the consequences of these events imaginable to most people. But "the pill" and AIDS serve in the popular imagination as the watershed developments that catalyzed and then killed the sexual revolution.

Measuring Sex

It is not entirely clear, however, that a discrete "sexual revolution" is anything more than a cultural artifact. Although there is clearly a countervailing trend toward more puritanical attitudes in some segments of society, the preponderance of evidence shows that sexual behavior has remained "loose"—and may even be continuing on a loosening trend—in the time of AIDS. . . .

The sexual revolution is such a contentious topic that even ostensibly objective social science gets tinged with the ideological predispositions of researchers. Though the data are now 50 years old, and though most experts believe its findings of sexual activity to be grossly inflated, the Kinsey reports remained the standard source for information about sexual activity until at least 1994. Various academic studies contradicted aspects of Kinsey's findings, but these studies were of much narrower scope. And broad studies of society that captured some data about sex, such as the General Social Survey (GSS), found quantities and varieties of sexual activity much lower than what Kinsey found. Would-be exegetes of the sexual revolution and its aftermath were left with a morass of conflicting and outdated information.

In 1993, Cynthia and Samuel Janus tried to rectify this situation, publishing *The Janus Report on Sexual Behavior,* for which they collected data between 1983 and 1992. Their findings only made things more confusing: They were unable to determine whether they were witnessing a backlash against the sexual revolution or a continuation of it. On the one hand the AIDS epidemic had made people claim to be more cautious about sex. On the other hand, they were having more sex with more people—especially among the most at-risk groups. Sixty-two percent of young men and 66 percent of young women reported that their sexual activity increased compared to three years earlier. Serious decline in sexual activity was shown by only 5 percent of the men and 9 percent of the women in the youngest group. Moreover, 24 percent of men and 20 percent of women reported "much more" sexual activity than three years earlier, and 44 percent of men and 41 percent of women reported "more" sexual activity. All told, 73 percent of men and 68 percent of women reported having the same or more sex in 1988–1992 than in 1985–1988.

Confronted with the conflicting data, the Januses weakly hedged their bets. This increase in sexual activity was, they said, the "Second Sexual Revolution." "The enormous tensions and backlash generated by these devastating sexually transmitted diseases made the practice of casual sex pause; from this hesitation, and the reaction to it, came the beginning of the Second Sexual Revolution." In other words, there was the revolution. Then there was the backlash against the revolution. Then there was the backlash against the backlash against the revolution. No wonder everyone is so confused.

Sex in America

The Janus report was based on a statistical sample of only 2,795, and many of the older respondents were found at sex-therapy clinics—so there is good reason to believe that many of their estimations of activity, like Kinsey's, are greatly overstated. But the following year another study appeared. Billed as the most comprehensive survey since Kinsey's, the National Health and Social Life Survey (NHSLS), popularly published as *Sex in America: A Definitive Survey*, dropped into American culture in 1994 like the original Kinsey report had nearly a half century earlier. Only while the Kinsey report had titillated and horrified with its previously unimaginable picture of sexual variety in the United States, *Sex in America* did quite the opposite.

What happened to the sexual revolution? *Sex in America* seemed to provide clear evidence that it was dead and gone, swept away by AIDS and a revival of sturdy family values. Some findings from its random sampling of 3,432 subjects: 94 percent of Americans were faithful to their spouses (up from around 60 percent in the Kinsey, Janus, and other surveys); only 33 percent of Americans had sex twice or more per week; the median number of lifetime sex partners for women was two, for men six. One of its more telling findings was that married people had the most sex, single people the next most, and divorced people the least. "The more partners you have," the report's authors wrote, "the more time you are going to spend finding and wooing them—time that a married couple could be having sex." In other words, if you like sex it doesn't pay to be a swinging single. Instead, get married and stay married. Our findings, the authors wrote, "often directly contradict what has become the conventional wisdom about sex. They are counterrevolutionary findings, showing a country . . . that, on the whole, is much less sexually active than we have come to believe." . . .

While the NHSLS's conclusions about sexual activity were generally much more conservative than the Janus report's, there were places where Janus's findings supported theirs. Though the NHSLS found that most young people did not have large numbers of sexual partners (more than 50 percent of 18- to 24-year-olds had just one partner in 1992), it also found that "the very sexually active people in the population, who are most at risk of being infected with HIV, did not seem to have been slowed by fears of AIDS." For example, 8.7 percent of people aged 25 to 29 claimed to have had 21 or more partners since age 18; 11.5 percent of 30- to 39-year-olds claimed to have had that many. The authors point out that if fear of AIDS had affected sexual activity, the highly promiscuous proportion of the younger group, who came of age after the explosion of AIDS, ought to have been much lower than it was relative to the older group.

But the most recent sex studies tell a more heartening story. On May 1, 1997, the National Survey of Family Growth, a government survey conducted every five years, released its most recent data, collected during 1995: The data showed that, for the first time since 1970, the percentage of teenagers having sex had declined. The percentage of girls aged 15 to 19 having sex declined from 55 to 50 between 1990 and 1995 (the number of married teenagers is so small these days, that even if marital sex is excluded, the percentage of girls having sex in 1995 falls by only 2 percent); and 55 percent of teenage boys had sex in 1995, down from 60 percent in 1988. Conservatives, no doubt, will take this as evidence that the sexual counterrevolution is, albeit slowly, taking hold. (And many adults think it should be taking hold faster; a March 1997 survey found that 95 percent of people surveyed believe teens should be completely abstinent.) But while something of a conservative sexual counterrevolution may finally be trickling down to younger Americans, the most encouraging data vindicate liberal sex-education policies: Condom use among young women has risen sharply, from 18 percent in the 1970s to 36 percent in the 1980s to 54 percent in 1995; in 1995, 91 percent of women said they had been taught safe-sex methods of preventing AIDS transmission. If condom use is up while sexual activity is down, then the conservative argument that sex education and contraception availability increase "immoral" and dangerous promiscuity looks less credible.

Who Won the Sexual Revolution?

"Uninhibited sex," writes the conservative political scientist Harvey Mansfield in *Reassessing the Sixties*, "received a rude shock from the emergence of AIDS. Perhaps you should listen more carefully to the vague menaces of your mother . . . about what happens to people who do funny things for sex." Well, perhaps that's true—to a point. But then Mansfield continues, "Since the sixties, feminine modesty has reasserted itself, though partly in the guise of feminism. There are now plenty of nice girls . . . but they are confused, apologetic, and unsupported by social norms. What they get for advice is 'safe sex.'"

Mansfield's tone—with his derisive "under the guise of feminism" and his patronizing "nice girls"—gives away the conservative game here. What conservatives like Mansfield want is less a curb on sexual excess than a rolling back of the political gains that women (and gays) have won under the auspices of the sexual revolution. It is difficult, of course, to tie victories in the political and social realms directly to victories in the sexual realm—maybe a right to sexual assertiveness is directly linked to a right to political assertiveness and maybe it isn't. But at the very least the sexual revolution for women was bound up in the larger revolutionary changes of the period that led to an improvement in their social status. You can't have the one without the other. Conservatives like Mansfield and [the Reverend Jerry] Falwell would like to erase both.

Conservative Moral Messages

Mansfield's strategy for achieving this erasure is typical. In fact, it's roughly what *The Rules* [a 1995 book by Ellen Fein and Sherrie Schneider that offers advice for attracting a male mate] does. First, point out that sexual liberation had a tangible, "science"-based cost: AIDS and other STDs. Next, cast the net more widely so that if sexual liberation was associated with women's liberation, for example, and sexual liberation caused AIDS, then women's liberation caused AIDS. All forms of liberation and political change connected to the sixties and seventies get implicated in this way. Women's rights, gay rights, woman's right to choose, and the freedom to do what you like in the privacy of your own bedroom all get thrown out the window with the bathwater.

In 1885, the prestigious British scientific journal the *Lancet* published an article arguing that the best method for protecting the young against STDs was the "cultivation of purity"—was "purity" a scientific concept or a moral one? The ambiguous rhetoric of "purity," neither clearly scientific nor clearly moral, is what for so many years has enabled traditional conservatives to extract from biology and epidemiology moral messages that are broader than the science merits.

The sexual revolution eliminated some hypocrisy. Those who trace the ruination of society to the breakdown of sexual morality forget that the old sexual morality was honored in the breach as often as not. Sure, in 1960 colleges had curfews and sexually segregated dorms. But remember that even then—no matter if Kinsey significantly overstated things— when the curfew bell rang, the campus shrubbery would quiver as young men and women emerged frantically pulling up their pants and smoothing down their dresses ready to run back to their single-sex dorms. Failing to acknowledge this, the anti-fornication crusaders are either dishonest ([televangelists] Jimmy Swaggart, Jim Bakker) or totally lacking in self-awareness ([judge] Robert Bork). In *Slouching Towards Gomorrah: Modern Liberalism and American Decline*, Bork writes:

> One evening at a hotel in New York I flipped around the
> television channels. Suddenly there on the public access
> channel was a voluptuous young woman, naked, her body

oiled, writhing on the floor while fondling herself intimately. . . . I watched for some time—riveted by the sociological significance of it all.

The sociological significance? Right. If Bork had been confirmed as a Supreme Court justice, we can guess the Court might have taken a lot more pornography cases for careful review.

Do Not Abandon the Sexual Revolution

The sexual revolution may not, in an important sense, have been worth its costs. Most gay men, the group most galvanized by the sexual revolution, would not say that the considerable political gains and social acceptance they've won over the last few years was worth human losses now numbering in the hundreds of thousands. But they would not want to give up those political gains and social acceptance. The [Reign of] Terror did not nullify all that the French Revolution achieved. Similarly, the ravages of AIDS do not mean that we should now abandon the liberal advances won by the sexual revolution. Less sexually wanton, yes; safer sex, yes; but we should not give in to rhetorical appeals for an oppressive new puritanism.

Chronology

1948

Alfred Kinsey publishes his scientific study *Sexual Behavior in the Human Male.*

1953

Kinsey publishes *Sexual Behavior in the Human Female.* The first *Playboy* magazine is published.

1956

Grace Metalious's *Peyton Place,* a novel that graphically depicts women as sexually eager and challenges the current sexual double standard, becomes a bestseller.

1960

The Food and Drug Administration approves the prescription of Enovid, the first birth control pill.

1962

Helen Gurley Brown's best-selling *Sex and the Single Girl,* a brazen description of Brown's free-spirited, unmarried lifestyle, is released.

1963

Betty Friedan's *The Feminine Mystique,* one of the most influential feminist texts ever written, is published. The book sharply criticizes the limitation of women to domestic roles.

1964

Pope John Paul VI publishes the encyclical *Humane Vitae,* in which he states the Catholic Church's condemnation of birth control and abortion. Title VII of the Civil Rights Act is passed, prohibiting sex discrimination in the workplace.

1965

Jeff Poland and others stage a nude "wade-in" in San Francisco to promote the Sexual Freedom League, a group promoting sexual openness and opposing conservative values.

Helen Gurley Brown becomes editor in chief of *Cosmopolitan* magazine.

Lawrence Lipton's book *The Erotic Revolution* features detailed discussions of wife-swapping.

1966

The National Organization for Women (NOW) is founded.

1967

Robert Rimmer's widely read novel *The Harrad Experiment* openly endorses group marriage.

In the case of *Loving v. Virginia*, the Supreme Court rules that laws against interracial marriages are unconstitutional.

Newspaper and magazines coin the term "Summer of Love" after a groundswell of hippies come to San Francisco for music, "free love," and drugs.

1968

Rock musical *Hair*, featuring public nudity and counterculture values, opens on Broadway.

1969

Police in New York City's Greenwich Village raid the Stonewall Inn, a gay bar. The ensuing riots mark the first occurrence of a unified gay resistance to established laws.

Four hundred thousand people come to Bethel, New York, for the Woodstock Music and Art Fair—a spirited three-day event featuring widespread sex and drug usage while musicians such as the Grateful Dead, Jimi Hendrix, and Janis Joplin perform.

1970

Shulamith Firestone claims in her 1970 book *The Culture of Romance* that while the sexual revolution offers more sexual freedom, it also perpetuates the objectification of women.

1971

Gloria Steinem founds *Ms.* magazine, the only mass-market feminist magazine in history.

1972

Deep Throat becomes the first pornographic film to be legally distributed nationwide.

1973

The Supreme Court rules 7-2 in the case of *Roe v. Wade,* making abortion legal in the United States.

1981

A rare form of pneumonia is reported to have killed five young gay men in Los Angeles—the AIDS crisis begins in America.

For Further Research

Books

David Allyn, *Make Love, Not War: The Sexual Revolution, an Unfettered History.* New York: Little, Brown, 2000.

Jules Archer, *The Incredible Sixties: The Stormy Years That Changed America.* San Diego: Harcourt Brace Jovanovich, 1986.

Bernard Asbell, *The Pill: A Biography of the Drug That Changed the World.* New York: Random House, 1995.

Thomas Atkins, ed., *Sexuality in the Movies.* Bloomington: Indiana University Press, 1975.

Helen Gurley Brown, *Sex and the Single Girl.* New York: Bernard Geis Associates, 1962.

John R. Cavanagh, *The Popes, the Pill, and the People.* Milwaukee, WI: Bruce, 1965.

Morris Dickstein, *Gates of Eden: American Culture in the Sixties.* New York: Basic, 1977.

Joan Didion, *Slouching Toward Bethlehem.* New York: Farrar, Straus & Giroux, 1968.

Angela G. Dorenkamp, John F. McClymer, Mary M. Moynihan, and Arlene C. Vadum, eds., *Images of Women in American Popular Culture.* New York: Harcourt Brace Jovanovich, 1985.

Barbara Ehrenreich, *The Hearts of Men: American Dreams and the Flight from Commitment.* New York: Doubleday, 1983.

David Farber, *The Age of Great Dreams: America in the 1960s.* New York: Hill & Wang, 1994.

Deborah Felder, *A Century of Women.* Secaucus, NJ: Birch Lane, 1999.

Shulamith Firestone, *The Culture of Romance.* New York: Morrow, 1970.

Betty Friedan, *The Feminine Mystique.* New York: Norton, 1963.

David Garrow, *Liberty and Sexuality: The Making of* Roe v. Wade. New York: Macmillan, 1994.

Donald Porter Geddes, ed., *An Analysis of the Kinsey Reports on Sexual Behavior in the Human Male and Female.* New York: New American Library, 1954.

Linda Gordon, *Woman's Body, Woman's Right: Birth Control in America.* New York: Penguin, 1990.

John Heidenry, *What Wild Ecstasy: The Rise and Fall of the Sexual Revolution.* New York: Simon and Schuster, 1997.

Carolyn G. Heilbrun, *The Education of a Woman: The Life of Gloria Steinem.* New York: Dial, 1995.

Daniel Hurewitz, *Stepping Out: Nine Tours Through New York City's Gay and Lesbian Past.* New York: Holt, 1997.

Sheila Jeffreys, *Anticlimax: A Feminist Perspective on the Sexual Revolution.* London: Woman's Press, 1990.

Alfred Kinsey et al., *Sexual Behavior in the Human Female.* Philadelphia: Saunders, 1953.

Eric Marcus, ed., *Making History: The Struggle for Gay and Lesbian Equal Rights, 1945–1990; An Oral History.* New York: HarperCollins, 1993.

Loretta McLaughlin, *The Pill, John Rock, and the Church: The Biography of a Revolution.* Boston: Little, Brown, 1982.

Kate Millet, *Sexual Politics.* New York: Simon and Schuster, 1970.

Ethan Morden, *Medium Cool: The Movies of the 1960s.* New York: Knopf, 1990.

George O'Neill and Nena O'Neill, *Open Marriage: A New Lifestyle for Couples.* New York: Avon, 1972.

Randy Shilts, *And the Band Played On: Politics, People, and the AIDS Epidemic.* New York: St. Martin's, 1987.

Rickie Sollinger, *Wake Up Little Susie: Single Pregnancy and Race Before* Roe v. Wade. New York: Routledge, 1992.

Taylor Stoehr, *Free Love in America: A Documentary History.* New York: AMS, 1979.

Elizabeth Siegel Watkins, *On the Pill: A Social History of Oral Contraceptives, 1950–1970.* Baltimore: Johns Hopkins University Press, 1998.

Periodicals

P. Abramson and B. Mechanic, "Sex and the Media: Three Decades of Best-Selling Books and Major Motion Pictures," *Archives of Sexual Behavior,* vol. 12, 1983.

Gilbert Bartrell, "Group Sex Among the Mid-Americans," *Journal of Sex Research,* May 1970.

Robert Bell and Jay Chaskes, "Premarital Sexual Experiences Among Coeds, 1958–1968," *Journal of Marriage and the Family,* vol. 32, 1970.

Ann Marie Cunningham, "The Pill: How It Changed Our Lives," *Ladies Home Journal,* June 1990.

Duane Denfield and Michael Gordon, "The Sociology of Mate Swapping; Or, the Family That Swings Together Clings Together," *Journal of Sex Research,* May 1970.

David Halberstam, "Discovering Sex," *American Heritage,* May/June 1993.

Caitlin Manning, "Whatever Happened to the Sexual Revolution?" *Socialist Review,* January/February 1987.

L. McLaughlin, "Dr. Rock and the Birth of the Pill," *Yankee,* September 1990.

Ira Robinson, "Twenty Years of the Sexual Revolution, 1965–1985: An Update," *Journal of Marriage and the Family,* February 1991.

Rod Stodghill II, "Where'd You Learn That?" *Time,* June 15, 1998.

Carolyn Symonds, "Sexual Mate Swapping and the Swingers," *Marriage Counseling Quarterly,* Spring 1971.

Web Sites

American Experience: The Pill (www.pbs.org/wgbh/amex/pill). This site explores the story behind the development of the birth control pill and features interviews, images, time lines, articles, and forums.

Human Rights Campaign (www.hrc.org). The largest national political organization devoted to working for equal rights for lesbian, gay, bisexual, and transgendered people.

The Kinsey Institute (www.indiana.edu/~kinsey). The Kinsey Institute promotes interdisciplinary research and scholarship in the fields of human sexuality, gender, and reproduction.

National Organization for Women (www.now.org). The extensive Web site of the organization Betty Friedan helped found in 1966 provides information on women's issues for women's rights activists.

The Summer of Love Mainpage (www.summeroflove.org). A Web site dedicated to chronicling the Summer of Love and its political accomplishments. It features articles and numerous photos.

Index

eliminated some hypocrisy,
132–33
men as beneficiaries of,
116–17
severed links between sex and
morality, 121–22, 124
women's opinions on, 115–
16, 118–19
Sloan, Sam, 53
*Slouching Towards Gomorrah:
Modern Liberalism and American
Decline* (Bork), 132
Sorokin, Pitirim A., 97
Spillane, Mickey, 102
Stanford Sexual Freedom Forum,
53
Steinem, Gloria, 66, 69
Stengel, Richard, 13
Stonewall Inn, 78
Stonewall Riots (1969), 77, 79
Stossel, Scott, 125
student activism, 53–54
surveys, 121, 123
on sexual activity, 128–30

Time (magazine), 58

Van Dusen, Henry Pitney, 30, 31,
32
Village Voice (newspaper), 81

Wall Street Journal (newspaper),
123
Wasted (Wolfe), 114
Watkins, Elizabeth Siegel, 56, 57
Wells, Herman, 28
White, Edmund, 110
Wicker, Randy, 47, 49
Wolfe, Linda, 114
women
changing domestic roles of,
122–23
prejudice against, in job market, 36–37
single, 20–22
women's movement, 15–16
goals of, 70–72
impact of, on lesbians coming out, 83, 87–88
societal benefits of, 74–76
Woodhull, Victoria, 46
Wylie, Sam, 45